WITHDRAWN

VanDerZee

PHOTOGRAPHER
1886 · 1983

VanDerZee

PHOTOGRAPHER
1886 · 1983

DEBORAH WILLIS-BRAITHWAITE

BIOGRAPHICAL ESSAY BY RODGER C. BIRT

HARRY N. ABRAMS, INC., PUBLISHERS
IN ASSOCIATION WITH
THE NATIONAL PORTRAIT GALLERY,
SMITHSONIAN INSTITUTION

VanDerZee, Photographer: 1886–1983 is published on the occasion
of an exhibition at the National Portrait Gallery, Smithsonian
Institution, Washington, D.C., October 22, 1993–February 13, 1994

Lenders to the Exhibition

Amon Carter Museum, Fort Worth, Texas
Anthony Barboza Photos, New York City
Consolidated Freightways, Inc., Palo Alto, California
Howard Greenberg Gallery, New York City
Alfred Forrest and Eloise Skelton-Forrest
Spike Lee
Terry Mansky
Martin Fine Art Photography, Chevy Chase, Maryland
The Metropolitan Museum of Art, New York City
The Museum of Modern Art, New York City
Dr. Regenia A. Perry
Prairie View A&M University, Texas
The Studio Museum in Harlem, New York City
Donna Mussenden VanDerZee

Page 2: *Self-portrait*, 1922. Donna Mussenden VanDerZee

PROJECT MANAGERS:
BEVERLY JONES COX, ERIC HIMMEL, AND NAOMI WARNER

DESIGNER:
RAYMOND P. HOOPER

Library of Congress Cataloging-in-Publication Data

Willis-Thomas, Deborah, 1948–
VanDerZee: photographer, 1886–1983/
Deborah Willis-Braithwaite;
biographical essay by Rodger C. Birt.
p.   cm.
"In association with the National Portrait Gallery, Smithsonian Institution."
Includes bibliographical references and index.
ISBN 0–8109–3923–1
1. Portrait photography—Exhibitions.   2. Afro-Americans—New York
(N.Y.)—Portraits—Exhibitions.   3. Harlem (New York, N.Y.)—Social
life and customs—Pictorial works—Exhibitions.   4. Van Der Zee,
James, 1886–1983—Exhibitions.   I. Title.
TR680.W54 1993
779′.2′092—dc20   93–18307
                                                          CIP

Published in 1993 by Harry N. Abrams, Incorporated, New York
A Times Mirror Company

Printed and bound in Japan

C O N T E N T S

Almost from the day he opened a studio in Harlem in 1912, James VanDerZee attained a local reputation that lasted for more than two decades. After World War II, clients proved hard to come by, and his work went into eclipse. It only became known to a wider audience through the controversial exhibition "Harlem On My Mind," which took place at the Metropolitan Museum of Art in New York in 1969, when the artist was eighty-two years old. Since then a selected portion of VanDerZee's work has become familiar. Now, at last, we are privileged to be able to see his career from start to finish, and to fully comprehend the considerable achievement that emerged from his long, productive life.

Over the past several years, the National Portrait Gallery has devoted a series of exhibitions to the work of individual photographers. Photographic portraits by Carl Van Vechten, Irving Penn, Annie Leibovitz, Arnold Newman, Richard Avedon, Julia Margaret Cameron, Mathew Brady (and his studio), and the pioneer daguerreotypist Robert Cornelius have been gathered to show how approaches to a familiar genre can vary. Each of these exhibitions had in common work of high quality and individuality, and each dealt (at least in part) with the depiction of nationally recognizable subjects. Even if judged only by these criteria, the work of James VanDerZee fully merits inclusion in this series.

But VanDerZee brings other dimensions into the picture, making this collection of work fundamentally different from any other we have explored so far. He was an African American. Camera and film may be color-blind, but sitters and publishers are not; surely VanDerZee brought a special insight into the lives and feelings of his subjects, while the nature of the commissions he received forced him to develop an eloquent and individual mode of expression. And the breadth of his experiences, from a comparatively sheltered childhood in small-town New England to his stimulating confrontation with the Harlem Renaissance, surely informed his aesthetic sensibility and his iconography.

Moreover, he placed his subjects recognizably in the context of their community, photographing them in life at home, in death at the church or funeral parlor, and in activity in the streets, clubs, and businesses of Harlem. These are not portraits taken against the total neutrality of a seamless-paper background, or in an unidentifiable corner. Even in his studio portraits, articles of clothing, works of art, or furnishings are often present to remind the viewer of the shared personal tastes and interests of photographer and subject. For the first time, the National Portrait Gallery looks at a community seen through the eyes of an insider; we are privy to the joys of new life, marriage, and accomplishment as well as to the pain of loss; we learn what is important, who is fashionable, and who is powerful.

These remarkable insights could never have been shared without the wholehearted cooperation of James VanDerZee's widow, Donna Mussenden VanDerZee, or without the passionate dedication of Deborah Willis-Braithwaite, who selected the photographs, and Roshini Kempadoo, Cheryl Finley, and Mecca Brooks, who assisted with the research. When Naomi Warner and Eric Himmel of Harry N. Abrams Publishers told us at the National Portrait Gallery about this project, we were immediately enthusiastic, and now we express our gratitude to the publisher for the production of this handsome volume. Rodger C. Birt, who is working on a definitive biography of VanDerZee, has eloquently shared his knowledge with us. Naomi Nelson, at the Studio Museum in Harlem, helped search through the thousands of negatives collected there. And we are deeply appreciative of the generosity of the institutional and private lenders who have allowed the use of vintage prints in their possession.

Most of all, we must be grateful to the late James VanDerZee himself for having created this body of work, unique in American photography, with special eyes, recording a time, a place, and a culture that we can recapture so vividly through the persistence of his vision.

Alan Fern
Director, National Portrait Gallery

THEY KNEW THEIR NAMES

DEBORAH WILLIS-BRAITHWAITE

Since the rediscovery of James VanDer-Zee's photographic archives in 1969, when his photographs were included in the Metropolitan Museum of Art's controversial exhibition "Harlem On My Mind," VanDerZee's images of the people of Harlem have been celebrated as an important and beautiful historic document. If, in the years since, critics and historians have come to value them primarily as a visual record of the emergence in America of the African American middle and upper classes, we should not be surprised, but we should not let this judgment limit our responses to the photographs themselves. It is ironic that this photographer, whose style it was to be extremely directorial, should be esteemed as a neutral observer of his times.

During the 1920s and 1930s, VanDerZee — a commercial portrait and street photographer — was indeed the photographer of choice for Harlem's most distinguished residents. Included in his archives, for example, among hundreds of prints and negatives of African Americans of comfortable means dating from the years between the wars, are photographs of World War I heroes Henry Johnson and Needham Roberts; singers Mamie Smith, Hazel Scott, and Florence Mills; poet Countee Cullen; and heavyweight boxing champions Jack Johnson, Harry Wills, Sam Langford, and Joe Louis. He was hired to photograph the major political and religious leaders of the period, such as Adam Clayton Powell, Sr., Adam Clayton Powell, Jr., Father Divine, Daddy Grace, George Becton, Rabbi Matthew, and the Barefoot Prophet. In 1924 he was made the official photographer for Marcus Garvey and the Universal Negro Improvement Association, in which capacity he created the most comprehensive visual record of that organization's activities in photographs that were published internationally in *The Negro World*, the UNIA newspaper.

Yet, to consider James VanDerZee's photographs primarily as historical documents — which is what the organizers of "Harlem On My Mind" did, inciting many in the Harlem community to protest that a museum ostensibly dedicated to art suddenly adopted a documentary stance when confronted with the visual presence of the "other" within its walls — is to overlook his contribution to photography as a form of expression. As critic A. D. Coleman had already observed in 1971, commenting on this ostensibly conventional commercial photographer's elaborate and handsome prints,

some of which combined images from several negatives, VanDerZee "goes beyond mere professional expertise, suggesting a concern with the aesthetic impact of his images which is significant in our evaluation of his work." Accepting at face value the photographer's own assertion that he "was both self-taught and, by his own admission, entirely out of touch with the aesthetic movements of his day in the photographic world," Coleman professed to be astonished by VanDerZee's high level of aesthetic sophistication.[1]

VanDerZee's photographs are widely known through numerous exhibitions and through three published monographs. While they have been acknowledged as a sweeping survey of the most vital pre–World War II African American community existing in the United States, VanDerZee has never been seen as the innovative photographic artist that he was. There has been virtually no critical analysis that describes the ideals that VanDerZee brought to and was able to express within his photography. This omission is, in part, due to the fact that viewers are often challenged, engaged, and overwhelmed by VanDerZee's subject matter, for his photographs are an overt celebration of black middle-class life, and particularly family life.

It is this picturing of middle-class life that gives VanDerZee's images much of their power to enchant and engage the viewer. Many of VanDerZee's portraits utilized the conventions and forms of studio portrait photography as they evolved in the second half of the nineteenth century in thousands of small photography businesses, a style created for clients who valued their dignity, independence, and comfort: they were formal and carefully composed works, and like the bourgeois and the celebrities in the photographs of the French photographer Nadar (1820–1910), their subjects are often made to appear both heroic and self-aware.

Yet, given the violent and tragic history of African Americans in the United States, this sense of self and self-worth, so apparent in VanDerZee's portraits, has a wholly other meaning than it does for the subjects of Nadar's photographs. VanDerZee's photographs — like the majority of photographic works associated with European and American modernism, with which they otherwise have little in common — were responses to the political and social upheavals of the early twentieth century. Like August Sander's massive photographic survey of pre–World War II Germans, VanDerZee's images define a people in the process of transformation and a culture in transition. Unlike Sander, who was obsessed with the representation of class structure and so-called "types," VanDerZee presented in visual terms the growing sense of personal, and national, identity of his sitters. Underpinning this is the thoroughly modern sensibility with which he confronted the issue of race. The conventional ideals of the bourgeois portrait studio served him well as a means to capture the culturally integrationist aspirations of his black clients. We might be tempted to call VanDerZee's work "radical" in the sense that the cultural critic and scholar bell hooks intends when she writes, regarding the representations of blacks in American culture, "Unless

we transform images of blackness, of black people, our ways of looking and our ways of being seen, we cannot make radical interventions that will fundamentally alter our situation."[2] VanDerZee's photography wrought one transformation on the image of blackness in America, and it is indeed possible to believe that for many, to be the subject of a VanDerZee photograph might be to experience a radical intervention in one's life, just as the rediscovery of his work in the late 1960s led many in the African American community to feel that a radical intervention had taken place in the historical record. It is this transformative power in his work that made VanDerZee a model of the visionary and optimistic early-twentieth-century American photographer.

In VanDerZee's work, this transformation takes the form of depicting people with a cosmopolitan style that, in the words of Mary Schmidt Campbell, was "partially real pride and partially carefully constructed artifice."[3] The sitter provided the pride, and VanDerZee provided the artifice. VanDerZee's photographs suggest that the waves of African American immigration from the Caribbean and the migration from the rural South to the cities of the North forever changed the visual self-image of the people who made the journey: they have been metamorphosed into suave and aware big-city dwellers; the degradations of the past have been seemingly eliminated from their present lives. In one striking photograph that could stand

ABOVE LEFT:
Woman in Fur-Trimmed Coat, 1928
The Metropolitan Museum of Art, New York City; gift of the James VanDerZee Institute, 1970 (1970.539.36)

ABOVE:
Man with cane, 1930
Donna Mussenden VanDerZee

A couple wearing raccoon coats with a Cadillac, taken on West 127th Street, 1932
Consolidated Freightways Collection, Palo Alto, California

for all the rest, an attractive couple dressed in matching raccoon coats poses with a beautiful Cadillac roadster. The passenger door is open, the man is half in the car itself, and the woman is standing next to it on the street, as if they are waiting patiently for the photographer to finish his work before they depart. But the man is not quite ready to leave: literally at the center of the image, framed by the luxurious automobile, he has turned his eyes directly into the lens, inviting the viewer to join them for a moment in their world. And this photograph, it is worth remarking, was made in 1932, fully three years after the stock market crash that signaled the beginning of the depression. In viewing VanDerZee's photographs taken in Harlem between the wars, one receives a sense of well-being and a feeling that the African American community is healthy, diverse, spiritual, prosperous, and productive.

We tend to think of VanDerZee as an observer, as a recorder, of the drama that we call the Harlem Renaissance, the decade-long (1919–29) flowering of African American art and culture in Harlem, but it might be more faithful to his role in it to think of him as one of its creators. His portraits of handsome men and beautiful women can be viewed as the visual embodi-

The Last Good-bye — Overseas,
1923
Donna Mussenden VanDerZee

The funeral of Blanche Powell,
Abyssinian Baptist Church, 1926
Donna Mussenden VanDerZee

they were still alive, to express their continuing presence in the lives of their loved ones. In the 1926 photograph of the funeral of Blanche Powell, the daughter of Adam Clayton Powell, Sr., a smiling image of the deceased girl hovers above the congregation of the Abyssinian Baptist Church in a manner that suggests that the spirit lives on after the body is broken. We know of no one else who photographed the rites of the dead so imaginatively, although postmortem photography has been widely practiced throughout American history. Such photographs must have had a special resonance in a Harlem where Victorian spiritual sentiment still found many eager adherents.

The main technique VanDerZee used in his mortuary photographs was photomontage, which involved using more than one negative to make a single photograph. The practice — called "combination printing" — was already established in art photography of the late nineteenth century. VanDerZee, as we have seen, always claimed to have had no exposure to mainstream art photography, but by World War I, photomontage was being used in the mass media, particularly in movies and advertising, and he would certainly have been aware of the convention of using ghostly images of loved

ABOVE:
Mortuary portrait of Florence Mills, 1927
Donna Mussenden VanDerZee

LEFT:
Unfinished mortuary portrait of Florence Mills, 1927
Donna Mussenden VanDerZee

Singer Florence Mills died of peritonitis in the fall of 1927 at the age of thirty-two, and the Harlem community gave her its most magnificent funeral. Her body lay in state for a week in the chapel of the Howell Undertaking Parlors at 137th Street and Seventh Avenue, where VanDerZee undoubtedly took this photograph. He had also made a portrait of the star earlier that year (see page 116).

ones in photographs to evoke spirits of the dead communicating with the living. His explanation of why he used the convention was characteristically expressive of his need to push the medium beyond the limitations inherent in straight photography: "I guess it was just a matter of not being satisfied with what the camera was doing. I wanted to make the camera take what I thought should be there, too."[5] A 1927 mortuary portrait of singer and comedienne Florence Mills reveals his working methods and his sense of photographic construction: in a work print, Mills's portrait is first placed in the upper right of the photograph above her coffin; in the final version of the photograph, Mills looks through the window of the chapel at her own corpse, in a way that suggests both the liberation of the soul and the contemplation of mortality.

The foregoing examples show VanDerZee manipulating symbols to establish a set of associations or ideas in the viewer's mind and to get at some essential truth about his subject. For VanDerZee, who had considerable early training in art and music, studio photography seems to have been a form of theater; an opportunity to "tell a story" with deliberately fictionalized elements. This led him to the exploration of startling and slightly surrealistic avenues that only opened up for mainstream "art photographers" in the 1980s. In one 1925 photograph, a father and son bundled up in winter clothes are posed in front of a backdrop painted with a snowy landscape, a rather unusual choice of setting given that most photographers using a backdrop of an outdoor scene would probably opt for something a little less ordinary and more exotic. More curious still is the well-known nude study — made for one of the calendars that VanDerZee published over the years — showing a young woman looking pensively into a fireplace, the very picture of a domesticized sensuality. That her skin glows in the warm light of

OPPOSITE AND ABOVE:
Couple posed in front of various studio backdrops, 1925
Donna Mussenden VanDerZee

In these photographs, VanDer-Zee used the same couple to try out various sentimental poses. A handwritten note on the first in the series reads, "When flowers means love and love means you."

Daydreams, 1925
The Studio Museum in Harlem Archives, James VanDerZee Photographic Collection; and the Donna VanDerZee Collection

VanDerZee's work with the couple in the previous series of photographs finally came to fruition in *Daydreams,* a more ambitious image that was probably developed for use in a calendar.

ABOVE:
Portrait of a man with his young son, posed before a winter backdrop, 1925
Donna Mussenden VanDerZee

RIGHT:
Future Expectations (Wedding Day), 1926
Donna Mussenden VanDerZee

OPPOSITE:
Nude, 1923
The Metropolitan Museum of Art, New York City; gift of the James VanDerZee Institute, 1970 (1970.539.27)

VanDerZee occasionally asked his clients if they wouldn't mind posing for calendar photographs, including nudes: " I don't say they came in particularly to make nude pictures but they had other pictures made, and I thought they'd make good subjects, and I got the pictures. . . . There was no difficulty to make these pictures because my wife was there too, and she'd just undress them and put them up in the pose there and then I'd set up the camera and make the pose."[93]

the fire is a tribute to VanDerZee's subtle control of studio lighting, for the fireplace with its cheery blaze is nothing more than a backdrop — visible in the photograph *Future Expectations* as well — painted by VanDerZee and Eddie Elcha, a fellow Harlem photographer. The convention of using painted backdrops was a staple of turn-of-the-century portrait-studio photography, but we would have to look far and wide for a photographer who pushed it so far as to have a model warming herself before a picture of a fire.

When VanDerZee's work was rediscovered in the late 1960s, serious American photography as it impinged on the African American community was largely focused on the amelioration of social problems. One way to understand more clearly who VanDerZee was and what he was about is to look at his work in relation to the documentary photographs produced in Harlem in the 1930s and 1940s by Aaron Siskind. Unlike VanDerZee's photographs, in

which the community of Harlem seems complete and self-contained, Siskind's images seem to define it in relation to the oppressive forces of the larger culture. Because the school of photography with which Siskind at this point in his career became associated helped to define and codify the social and political conditions of the disadvantaged — the poor, the unemployed, the victims of racism, the "forgotten" members of society — and because their work itself seemed to be at least partially motivated by "social consciousness," such photographers became known as "concerned photographers." It is clear that VanDerZee does not belong among them, and VanDerZee's work would appear naive to anyone accustomed to viewing a place like Harlem through their lenses.

Curiously, like VanDerZee's, Siskind's Harlem photographs, taken between 1932 and 1940, were not published as a group until long after World War II, in Siskind's case not until 1981. It is possible to imagine the two of them running into one another at a street demonstration, each with their large-format camera and tripod, coming together fortuitously from their different worlds. Born and raised in New York City, Siskind (1903–1992) became interested in photography in 1930 while working as an English teacher in a city public school, and he quickly joined the New York Worker's Film and Photo League. The Film and Photo League was formed in 1929 as a political organization that utilized photography and film as tools in promoting class struggle and social reform. Its original purpose was to provide photographs for the left-wing press, such as the *Daily Worker* and the *New Masses*, and to create silent newsreels on themes like unemployment and hunger. In 1936, the group split because of clashes between members who believed solely in its political mission and those, branded "elitists" by the others, who, even though they shared a conviction that art should foster social change, wanted to be free to explore aesthetic issues as well. Siskind, who was in the latter camp, became a leading member of the group it formed, which was called simply the Photo League, and he was instrumental in setting up a smaller documentary production unit within the league called the Feature Group. The Feature Group created photographic essays documenting the impact of the depression in various facets of American life.

Siskind's Harlem photographs were created for two different projects. In 1936 Michael Carter, an African American writer, approached the eight photographers in the Feature Group with the idea of creating a document of Harlem. Photographs Siskind made from 1932 to 1936 were included in the final work, which was completed in 1939 but never published (there was an exhibition, and some of the photographs appeared in *Fortune* and *Look*). In 1940 Siskind, along with photographer Max Yavno and Carter, began another project called "The Most Crowded Block," which they left incomplete when Yavno was drafted in 1941 and Siskind's interests began to shift away from documentary photography toward the more formal, abstract work for which he became known. Many of these powerfully constructed images, created on Harlem's streets and in its nightclubs and churches, suggest how an outsider could conceive of Harlem's residents as the "oppressed other." Certainly, the economics of the 1930s changed the character of the Harlem community, which accounts in part for the pessimistic tone of Siskind's images: By 1937 the unemployment rate for African Americans

OPPOSITE ABOVE LEFT:
Aaron Siskind. *Mother and Daughter at Dinner*, circa 1935
National Museum of American Art, Smithsonian Institution, Washington, D.C.; gift of Tennyson and Fern Schad, Courtesy Light Gallery

OPPOSITE ABOVE RIGHT:
Aaron Siskind. *Untitled*, date unknown
National Museum of American Art, Smithsonian Institution, Washington, D.C.

OPPOSITE BELOW:
Black Cross nurses, 1924
The Studio Museum in Harlem Archives, James VanDerZee Photographic Collection; and the Donna VanDerZee Collection

was at least three times that of whites. Yet, by comparing VanDerZee's and Siskind's views of Harlem, two separate and distinct notions of the vitality of the African American community emerge. While VanDerZee's best photographs seem to celebrate a sense of self-identity and racial pride, Siskind's most powerful works deal with notions of class distinction and racial segregation. Unlike VanDerZee's photographs, which picture the community as whole and functioning, Siskind was concerned with how racism and poverty defined the character of Harlem. Simply stated, to VanDerZee Harlem was home; to Siskind it was a ghetto.

VanDerZee's camera takes the viewer into the same places that Siskind does, but the sadness and longing of Siskind's photographs are absent from VanDerZee's. Part of this is due to Siskind's method of constructing his images. While no one can be unobtrusive with a view camera, Siskind often gives the impression of photographing people who are unaware of his presence and sometimes surprising his subjects, who seem irritated by the intrusion. In Siskind's images, the main subject is often isolated or surrounded by the artifacts of poverty. In his use of sharp camera angles and image-cropping, Siskind created a sense of dislocation that suggests alienation from the larger culture. Many of Siskind's images were taken from above, suggesting the photographer's and society's distance from the subjects. VanDerZee's photographs, on the other hand, even those made on Harlem's streets, are formal images containing aspects of both ceremony and ritual. They are crowded with people engaged in mutual pursuits, suggesting shared values, aspirations, and goals.

One of Siskind's photographs of the early 1930s shows a woman marching in a street parade. Her clothing identifies her as a member of Father Divine's religious and social movement. She is positioned in the right front half of the picture frame and is dressed differently and separated physically from two other women also visible in the photograph, all of which makes her seem removed from the march. Even though she looks directly at the viewer, her gaze is confrontational and abstracted. The march itself seems futile.

VanDerZee's photographs of the many parades and demonstrations in Harlem, on the other hand, often have a celebratory feeling about them. In one of his 1924 photographs for the UNIA, a line of Black Cross nurses carry signs that contain political messages. The group fills the entire picture frame, suggesting a massive gathering. This photograph differs in feeling from Siskind's image because the women interact and smile at each other in the shared joy and responsibility of having a mutual purpose and goal.

Since VanDerZee needed to generate future commissions, it was to his economic advantage to represent Harlem and its people in the best possible light. His success as a commercial photographer was predicated not only on his pleasing his clients but also on their economic success. But VanDerZee's Harlem photographs and Siskind's Harlem Document, as the project came to be called, cannot be summed up as simply a positive versus a negative view of the community: one created for commercial reasons and the other for social protest. Although the latter are often stark and beautiful, VanDerZee's photographs actually reveal more about the nature of Harlem. This is the genius in VanDerZee's work. His images speak of the liveliness of the community and its capacity for renewal, its constant reinvention of itself, and its growth. In contrast, Harlem Document and the countless documentary essays that followed it have as their foundation a sense of alienation and victimization.

VanDerZee's photographs are about the connection between self and family and self and community. James Baldwin, writing about the residents of Harlem in his memoir *Nobody Knows My Name*, suggested that "They struggle to instill in their children some sense of dignity which will help the child to survive. This means, of course, that they must struggle, solidly, incessantly to keep this sense alive in themselves."[6] The fruits of this struggle are missing from most documentary imagery of African American life in the 1930s and 1940s; they can be found, for obvious reasons, in the photographs of the civil rights movement.

Because VanDerZee's work was largely absent from public view for several decades, it was not known to the generations of photographers that came of age after the 1940s, for whom it might have made a difference. His secure, middle-class upbringing gave him an invaluable perspective on African American life and culture, enabling him to make photographs that were removed from what came to be, by the depression, the predominant and accepted way of depicting the African American experience in photographs. What has always distinguished the middle classes is a strong, autonomous sense of self, and this VanDerZee both had for himself and was able to recognize in his subjects.

Nor was the photographic establishment particularly sympathetic to VanDerZee's aesthetic approach to the medium of photography, nurtured as it was by his artistic temperament and early training in art and music, when the work was first presented to a wide public in the 1970s. Today, however, that establishment has arrived at a view of photography that is far more inclusive of different modes of expression, and many of the techniques that VanDerZee used — the *mise-en-scène*, photomontage, the manipulation of the image through retouching — have gained wide acceptance.

VanDerZee's photographs can be considered the foundation for much of the subjective and self-referential work currently being produced by African American photographers like Dawoud Bey, Jeffrey Scales, Roland Freeman, Roland Charles, and Coreen Simpson, to name a few. The spiritual link between VanDerZee and contemporary artists has at its core the creation of a revisionist history of the African American experience that emphasizes family, community, and personal identity. In James VanDerZee's photographs the elusive and essential nature of the selfhood of African Americans is defined and contained.

A LIFE IN AMERICAN PHOTOGRAPHY

RODGER C. BIRT

Although James VanDerZee lived the last seventy-five years of his life in New York City and eventually became celebrated as the preeminent photographer of Harlem, he remained at heart a New Englander. During the three-quarters of the century he spent in New York, his manner, his sense of how life should be lived, even his slightly detectable accent all resonated with the rhythms of his small-town Massachusetts beginnings.

He came from the Berkshire mountain hamlet of Lenox, which was then known as the "inland Newport," a popular summer retreat for some of the wealthiest families in America.[7] Among the glamorous summer crowd of Morgans, Westinghouses, and Carnegies quietly stepped Egbertses, Osterhauts, Bristers, and VanDerZees, the local working-class black men and women who made their living providing the services that the wealthy residents of the summer estates paid handsomely for. During the first of many interviews he would give, VanDerZee said about Lenox that he "would like very much to go back."[8] And when he undertook his last great series of photographs, portraits of famous African Americans, it can be said that the genteel qualities of Gilded Age Lenox and the black community he was born into there informed his work.

James VanDerZee's maternal grandfather, William Egberts, first purchased property in Lenox in 1852. He came to Lenox from New Baltimore, New York. The land Egberts purchased was owned by Joseph Schermerhorn, also of New Baltimore. Egberts's lot was the first parcel of land on what would eventually become a large tract owned by members of the extended family that included Osterhauts, Bristers, and VanDerZees. William Egberts married Josephine Brister, a woman from nearby Stockbridge. Susan, their only child, was James VanDerZee's mother. After her first husband's death Josephine married again. Her second marriage also was to a man from across the mountains in New York. He was David Osterhaut, skilled at handling horses and, like William Egberts, an accomplished carpenter and farmer. Osterhaut prospered and became a leading member of the small local black community. The dozen or so black families scattered throughout the mountain towns maintained an informal network linking

OPPOSITE:
The VanDerZee men, Lenox,
circa 1909
Donna Mussenden VanDerZee

From left: James, Walter, John, and Charles

families in Lenox, Stockbridge, Pittsfield, and Great Barrington. In addition, the immigrants from New York State stayed in contact with friends and relatives who had remained in their Hudson River Valley hometowns.[9] In consequence, the members of the African American community in the Berkshires were much less insular than their white neighbors. An indication of this parochialism is to be found in the statement of one white Lenox resident who said, when departing for a trip across the Berkshires to Amsterdam, New York, that he was about to take a journey "out west."[10]

John VanDerZee, James's father, who moved to Lenox in the late 1870s or early 1880s, was another in the line of black migrants from New Baltimore. Like the young white men from the Hudson River Valley who left home in search of better jobs, usually in manufacturing and industrial centers like Rochester and Albany, John VanDerZee also sought improved economic prospects. However, while race prohibited his joining the new industrial labor force in New York State, jobs were plentiful in Lenox, where wealthy estate builders needed butlers, livery men, and skilled carpenters. So John VanDerZee, like William Egberts and David Osterhaut before him, crossed the mountains looking for work and found a wife. In 1882 he married Susan Elizabeth Egberts, Josephine Brister's daughter and David Osterhaut's stepdaughter. Not long after their marriage, John and Susan VanDerZee moved to New York City.

Both John and Susan were experienced servants, accustomed to working for the wealthy. For a while they worked, as maid and butler, for Ulysses S. Grant, the retired President and Civil War hero, who was then living in a Fifth Avenue mansion purchased by his political supporters and trying to win battles on Wall Street.[11] When Susan became pregnant, they decided to leave the metropolis and return to the calmer life of Lenox.

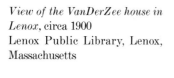

View of the VanDerZee house in Lenox, circa 1900
Lenox Public Library, Lenox, Massachusetts

Jane (1885–1956), whom everybody called Jennie, was the first born. She and James were close throughout their lives. James was born on June 29, 1886. A year and a half later came Samuel Walter (1887–1953), who preferred to be called Walter. He and James also enjoyed a warm fraternal bond. The younger brothers, John (1890–1896) and Charles (1892–1911), and sister Mary (1895–1911) were all loved, but the oldest three had a special relationship. To accommodate their growing family, the VanDerZees moved into a house situated between that of Lena Brister, Susan's aunt, and another that had recently been purchased by her mother and stepfather, Josephine and David Osterhaut. This would be their safe and secure haven for the next twenty years.

The childhood James, his sisters, and his brothers enjoyed in Lenox was comfortable and, in his own recollection, almost a bucolic ideal. They wanted for nothing; there was always enough money, and the family grew its own vegetables and fruit, raised livestock, and kept poultry. As VanDerZee recalls:

> We used to help father plant things in the garden. We needed a big garden because there were so many of us children. We had cows and horses and chickens. We grew up knowing a little bit about everything, how you put seeds in the ground, how in a few days you go out there and look and see a little sprout coming up. You nourish it, you rake the dirt up around the roots, and each day you see the corn and beans and all the different things grow a little bit more. . . . There was always plenty of wood for the fire in winter, plenty of food on the table at mealtimes.[12]

In the summer they rode their bicycles, went swimming, and ran errands for the adults who worked at the estates. By the end of September the wealthy summer visitors had mostly departed, and once again Lenox belonged to the year-round residents. In winter the family would seek out favorite spots for ice fishing, and the boys made pocket money clearing snow from sidewalks and porches.

The children were encouraged to excel at school and to pursue their intellectual and artistic interests. Jennie was the best student, while James was especially interested in the music and art classes. Their otherness, their not being of European ancestry, did have its disturbing moments. VanDerZee could never erase from memory one such occasion, which he vividly recounted seventy years after the event occurred.

> We were going to have a geography lesson, and I looked in the book and it said something like, "Africa is the hottest of all continents, it's the home of the Negro, or black race. They are known by their thick lips and kinky hair." And I didn't think I wanted to be present at school when that came up. So, my brother and I thought we'd take a walk to Pittsfield that day. Just our luck, they didn't have the lesson that day but the day after. One or two of the kids looked back at us because they felt we were the nearest to Africans.[13]

However, neither bigotry nor overt racial prejudice framed his memories of the Lenox years. He and his siblings enjoyed the love and security of a stable, successful, and large extended family. Their father was sexton at the Trinity Episcopal Church for a decade and a half, while their mother, grandmother, and aunts operated a bakery and laundry. Each member of the family either sang, played a musical instrument, or did both. James, whose first love was music, eventually became an accomplished violinist and piano player.

He was fascinated by images, VanDerZee said, since his earliest memories.[14] Reproductions in books, drawings provided by teachers, and pictures on the walls of his parents', aunts', and grandparents' homes all fascinated him. He showed talent at art and calligraphy and was often asked by teachers to provide artwork for the school. His interest in photography grew naturally as the logical development of his love for pictures of all kinds. Photography offered another means of making pictures. Intrigued by an advertisement that promised a camera as the prize for selling packets of ladies' sachet powder, he filled out and mailed off the coupon. First came the sachet powder, twenty packets. He sold them and returned the money to the advertiser's address. Several weeks later a camera, of sorts; a few glass plates; and an assortment of chemicals arrived. VanDerZee read the instructions and went to work. He pointed the camera at everything and everybody in sight and then, when all the plates had been exposed, he withdrew into the makeshift darkroom he had set up in the closet of his bedroom. Sadly, the experiment was a failure, and the young photographer had no photographs to show for his labors.[15] Nevertheless, his interest had been aroused, and he soon purchased a second camera from a mail-order company in New York with money he had saved from various odd jobs. By now it was in the spring of 1900, a few months before his fourteenth birthday and the last year he attended school. That summer he went to work, first in a local boardinghouse and then as a waiter in the Hotel Aspinwall, one of the luxury resort hotels that was opening in the Berkshires as Lenox and other nearby towns became tourist meccas for a well-to-do but less affluent clientele than the previous generation's estate builders. His father was also on the Aspinwall's staff of waiters, all of whom were black. Some of the men were college students making extra money before returning to campus. Others, like John VanDerZee, were career waiters, skilled at being what John called a "gentleman's gentleman."[16] While working at the Aspinwall, James continued to play the violin and piano and refine his photography.

The extant photographs of this period (1900–1904) are primarily family scenes and portraits of friends. They exhibit his early mastery of the basic photographic skills of exposure, development, and print making. In addition, VanDerZee's sensitive eye for the dramatic use of natural light and detail are also already apparent. One of the best examples from this period is the portrait of Mrs. Turner, one of Lenox's wealthy summer residents. It was during these years, after he left school and while he was working as a waiter

Mrs. Turner, Lenox, Massachusetts, 1905
Martin Fine Art Photography,
Chevy Chase, Maryland

at the Aspinwall, that VanDerZee discovered how rewarding photographs could be, not only as pictures but as marketable commodities. With the money he was now earning at the Aspinwall he decided to build a more extensive darkroom and set up a natural-light portrait studio in his parents' house, but during a verbal altercation with another employee of the hotel, VanDerZee lost his temper and struck the man. Unceremoniously, VanDer-Zee was discharged and plans for the new studio were dashed.[17] John Van-DerZee had already left Lenox for New York and was working in the dining room of the Knickerbocker Trust Bank. James and Walter decided to join their father. In 1905 they rode a series of interurban electric cars all the way from Lenox to Manhattan for the princely sum of three dollars and fifty cents. The wonderful New England boyhood was over.

II

In moving to New York, John VanDerZee had made an important decision; he would remain there and send for the family after he was established. By now he was in the early stages of the tuberculosis that ultimately would kill him, and the work at the Aspinwall and the Berkshire mountain winters had become too demanding. After his father left for New York, the family, James said, felt that it was "broke up."[18] Now that he and Walter also had departed, only the women and the younger children remained in Lenox. The patterns of life established when William Egberts and David Osterhaut moved to Lenox fifty years earlier remained unchanged there for the most part, and the pulse of the new century was still barely felt in the village. In New York, however, it was an exciting time.

The Lexington Avenue IRT had just recently been completed, and a second bridge across the East River was in the final stages of construction. In 1898 New York City had been expanded from Manhattan to include the four "outer boroughs," and the new transportation system to link the city was being put in place. The population was growing by several hundred thousand a year. Most of the new residents came from abroad, but their numbers were swelled by Americans like the VanDerZees who also looked to urban areas as they left the small towns and farms of their youth. In New York it was as if the world had rushed in. VanDerZee had never seen anything like it. He marveled at the number of shops and stores, and the large population of people of African descent. They came from everywhere, but most were from the southern United States. The city's pace was fast and intimidating, but it was also exhilarating.

James and Walter moved to the Tenderloin District, into the same boardinghouse on 24th Street near Seventh Avenue where their father resided. John helped them get jobs waiting tables in the Knickerbocker Trust dining room, and James later took a job as an elevator operator. There are no photographs from this period, but VanDerZee did continue playing music. He held a variety of music jobs: dancing schools, social club parties, and church benefits. It was at a church fund-raising event at St. Mark's Church that he met Kate L. Brown.

Kate was from Virginia and, as VanDerZee once reminisced, "that will win ya."[19] Photographs reveal a tall, thin, elegant woman with a delicate beauty. At their first meeting she approached VanDerZee to compliment him on his violin playing. He asked if he could see her again, and she agreed. He liked her but had only wanted a brief dalliance; when Kate became pregnant, VanDerZee felt that "the manly thing" to do was to marry her.[20] He had not wanted to marry yet, but he had been raised with an ethic that demanded he honor both the woman and his own responsibility. They were married in March 1907 and moved into an apartment on West 29th Street.

Both continued to work, Kate as a seamstress and VanDerZee as an

Kate VanDerZee, circa 1908
Donna Mussenden VanDerZee

elevator operator. But when Kate neared time to deliver, they decided, as had VanDerZee's parents, to have their child in Lenox. His mother, grand-mother, aunts, and sisters were still there in the three houses, and the secure life he remembered beckoned him home. They stayed in the upstairs bed-room that had been James's and Walter's when they were boys, and the child, Rachel (1907–1927), was born in September. After Thanksgiving it was time to visit Kate's relatives who lived in Phoebus, Virginia, near the en-trance to the Chesapeake Bay. The VanDerZees traveled by boat and arrived in time for Christmas. The journey to Virginia turned out to be more than just a visit to Kate's relatives. In Virginia VanDerZee returned to photogra-phy for the first time since his departure from Lenox in 1905.

Kate had an intimate knowledge of Phoebus and the surrounding neigh-borhood. She had spent several years there before going to New York, and she knew VanDerZee could find work in nearby Old Point Comfort. Phoebus was the residential enclave for the black population living on Hampton Roads, the narrow strait separating Phoebus from Norfolk. Phoebus was a newly incorporated town next to Fort Monroe, an important site in the early history of the Civil War. The fort had been headquarters for the Union Army in the Department of Eastern Virginia and North Carolina. During the war it became a haven for runaway slaves. The runaways erected a temporary shantytown of canvas tents and wooden shacks that was called Slabtown.[21] After the war the "contrabands," now free men and women, purchased lots in Slabtown and renamed it Chesapeake City. In 1900 Chesapeake City was renamed Phoebus, in honor of Harrison Phoebus, who had been instrumental in bringing the railroad to the region and who had owned and operated the old Hygeia Hotel and Spa. When VanDerZee and Kate arrived in 1908, the Hygeia had been demolished and replaced by a new, luxury hotel, the Chamberlin. The Chamberlin, as one writer quaintly put it, catered to "a most distinguished and interesting clientele . . . the select society of the successful."[22] VanDerZee knew who the members of that "select society" were. He had met them in Lenox at their summer estates and at the Aspinwall. More recently he had taken their lunch orders at the Knickerbocker Trust Bank. The Chamberlin, which had an all-black staff of five hundred, could always use an experienced waiter, and VanDerZee easily secured a position. The steady income and the relatively benign winter were inducements to stay. For Kate it was a homecoming.

VanDerZee was particularly attracted to the activities at Hampton Institute and the Whittier Preparatory Academy. The history of the two schools for black students went back to the 1860s. Hampton had been incorporated as the "Hampton Normal and Agricultural Institute for the instruction of youth in the various common school, academic and collegiate branches." Between 1878 and 1912 it also admitted Native Americans, who made up about 10 percent of the student body in the early 1900s.[23] Whittier Preparatory Academy, named for poet and abolitionist John Greenleaf Whittier, took students as young as six and seven and provided them with the basic education they would need to be successful at Hampton. Whittier Academy also offered music and art instruction for Hampton students and other adults.[24] VanDerZee enrolled in music classes at Whittier. He soon found that he was as accomplished a musician as were his would-be teachers. The local population embraced his musical virtuosity, as they had done in New York, and he was soon playing at community recitals and church socials. "I was a big professor down there," he recalled.[25] In addition to the musical performances and the work at the hotel, he started photographing again. He took his camera outdoors, onto campus lawns, into classrooms and homes of faculty members, and to the part of Phoebus still called Slabtown. The black community of Lenox had been by and large homogeneous: there was no poverty to speak of and no professional class. Only in New York had VanDerZee begun to see the wider variety of African American experiences. Living in Phoebus increased his knowledge of black America even more. Here was a community of successful black scholars living next door to black squalor. VanDerZee photographed both.

The Whittier photographs are all posed and possess a formality that, in

part, was dictated by the long exposure time that available light demanded.
The Slabtown photographs are more candid and have what contemporary
writers called an "instantaneous" quality. In the Slabtown work, the interest
is topographical, with human characters considered as part of the larger
tableaux. In contrast, the primary concern of the Whittier photographs is
the human subject. VanDerZee draws the viewer's attention to these people,
who they are, and what they value. The commitment of the young Whittier
scholars to their education and the modern classrooms is put on display in a
straightforward, documentary style. The photographs of the teachers, fre-

quently taken in their homes, are more intimate. Here, VanDerZee began to develop a subjective style and attention to interior details that look ahead to his studio portraits from the 1920s and 1930s. Even though the relatives of Kate they stayed with, the Jenkins family, came from Slabtown, VanDerZee was an outsider there, largely oblivious to its discomforting implications. Unlike Slabtown, the Whittier Academy — a world of domestic bliss and social orderliness — was familiar territory to VanDerZee, and if he could only coldly observe the former, it was natural that he should heroize the latter.

To a degree, however, VanDerZee was also an outsider at Whittier. Although he was addressed as "professor," a faculty position was not likely. He possessed the practical skills of both musician and photographer, but he had left high school before receiving his diploma. Then there were the indignities of the Jim Crow laws that even the most successful blacks of Phoebus had to suffer. VanDerZee never adjusted to segregation. After less than half a year the Phoebus interlude ended. The time there, however, had provided VanDerZee with an invaluable lesson: he could succeed as a musician and as a photographer, if not in Phoebus, then in New York. Early in spring 1908, VanDerZee and his family left Virginia.

III

Rather than return to one of the black West Side neighborhoods they knew (the Tenderloin or San Juan Hill), the VanDerZees chose to live in a part of the city only recently opened up to African Americans: Harlem. In the Colonial era, Harlem had been a sleepy farming community far to the north of the bustling city downtown. During the American Revolution it was the site of one great battle and many skirmishes between British and American forces. After the war, and well into the 1870s, Harlem was a favored retreat for wealthy families, who built country homes there. However, when the elevated commuter railroads pushed as far north as 129th Street in the 1870s, Harlem's isolation ended. During the next two decades speculators moved in and developed the Harlem countryside, erecting row upon row of townhouses and apartment buildings. Families of Irish, Italians, German Jews, and other European ethnic groups, all eager to escape slum and ghetto conditions downtown, purchased homes or leased apartments. For a while the speculators made a lot of money, but in the 1900s the bubble burst as renters and would-be purchasers were lured to the suburban environment of the "outer" boroughs newly accessible via subway and streetcar lines. Facing high vacancy rates, real-estate agents turned to another group of working-class New Yorkers who wanted to escape the dingy banality of crowded and decrepit tenement housing: they began to court the African American residents of San Juan Hill and the Tenderloin. The campaign of the entrepreneurs worked. By 1907 five out of ten Harlem residents were black and

they were his models; Kate's side of the marriage is lost to us. VanDerZee evidently hoped to use the family and its tradition of closeness to inspire his failing union with Kate, for in 1910, after his sister Jennie's marriage to Ernest Toussaint, all the VanDerZees gathered briefly together again, this time in New York City. Toussaint seemed to enjoy the presence of his extended family of in-laws, so John, Susan, and their two youngest children, Mary and Charles, moved in with Jennie and Ernest, while James, Walter, and their families took nearby apartments.

VanDerZee worked sporadically as a musician and even went as far as to form his own band, but photography remained a significant factor in his life. In 1911 he took a job as a photographic assistant in Newark, New Jersey. A photographer, Charles Gertz, who operated a portrait concession in Hahne's, Newark's biggest department store, wanted a darkroom technician. To avoid having to make the long commute from Manhattan to New Jersey, VanDerZee decided that he, Kate, and Rachel should move to Newark. Shortly after going to work for Gertz, VanDerZee graduated from the darkroom to the posing chambers. His skill at portraiture was evident both to Gertz and to the customers who requested that "the colored fellow" take their picture.[28] VanDerZee had been in Newark for less than a year when Jennie invited him to join her at the Toussaint Conservatory of Art and Music, which she had opened in 1911. She believed a portrait studio in conjunction with the music instruction and study would appeal to her clients. She suggested to James that he move back to New York and open a studio at the conservatory, and he readily accepted the offer. For one thing, his family needed him nearby now. In 1911, John VanDerZee succumbed to the tuberculosis he had been ill with for almost ten years, and shortly afterwards VanDerZee's younger sister and brother, Mary and Charles, died. His mother still lived with Jennie, and his return to Harlem would enable him to see her on a regular basis. He stayed at the conservatory from 1912 until 1915.

Among the photographs from this period are portraits of his cousin Susan Porter and Blanche Powell, daughter of Adam Clayton Powell, Sr., and sister of the future congressman. Whether he posed his subjects in a studio setting, as he did with Blanche Powell, or in their own surroundings, as with Susan Porter, VanDerZee did not allow setting to overpower persona. Both portraits demonstrate his ability to evoke a sense of the sitter's character in an effective and naturalistic manner. They also show his allegiance to pictorial conventions that commercial portrait photographers had been employing since the 1860s. The parlor in the Porter portrait and the arrangement of props in the Powell portrait have visual cognates found in *cartes des visites* and cabinet-card portraits made after the Civil War. Both photographs show how explicitly VanDerZee was working within Victorian and contemporary Edwardian traditions while at the Toussaint Conservatory. His studio practices during the years under discussion vary in no significant way from

Gaynella VanDerZee. *James VanDerZee*, 1931
Donna Mussenden VanDerZee

VanDerZee's instruments were the violin and the piano. He was first violin in the Wanamaker orchestra when he worked briefly at Wanamaker's on Fourth Street, and he later played in the orchestras at the Lincoln Theater (accompanying silent films), the Lafayette Theater, and the Apollo Theater in Harlem.

OPPOSITE:
Gaynella VanDerZee, circa 1918
Donna Mussenden VanDerZee

those utilized in thousands of studios throughout the United States. In effect, he was very much a part of the mainstream.[29]

VanDerZee's artistic achievements at the Toussaint Conservatory did not change Kate's mind. She still viewed photography as an economically uncertain sideline and admonished him to work at something that would provide a more certain income. He continued to work as an elevator operator, to wait tables and to take music engagements and give music lessons. He could not hold his family together, however, and in 1916 Kate decided to leave. Van-DerZee accepted the separation but accused Kate of leaving him for another man. The most difficult part was not being able to see the eight-year-old Rachel on a regular basis. He would miss her.

IV

The pain of the breakup was eased somewhat, however, by the new person who had come into VanDerZee's life. She worked as switchboard operator in the building where he operated the elevator. She was attractive, she enjoyed talking with him, and, perhaps most importantly, his work in photography intrigued her. Although she was married, Gaynella Greenlee had no reservations about letting VanDerZee know that she liked him.

Gaynella was of European ancestry; her father was born in Germany and her mother in Spain.[30] After she and VanDerZee married, she said, when asked, that she was a light-complexioned black woman. Only family members and a handful of their most intimate friends knew the truth. When

they met, her husband, Charles Greenlee, was an invalid and near death, living in Westchester with his parents. Meanwhile, Gaynella was alone in Manhattan and easily found the time to be with VanDerZee. Their conversations often came around to his plans for a studio. As they talked more, her joining him in the venture became a part of the imagined studio. Soon it was agreed to; they would have a studio together in Harlem. To avoid gossip about their not being married, they devised a ruse. "I let it appear that it was her studio and I was working for her," VanDerZee said.[31]

They called the studio, which opened in 1917, the Guarantee Photo Studio. It was located at 109 West 135th Street, next door to the West 135th Street Branch of the New York Public Library. This would be the first of four sites Gaynella and James would rent over the next twenty-five years. From the beginning the business was a success. Harlem's black population was now the majority. New institutions were forming while already established ones were undergoing conversion. Social clubs, athletic organizations, and church groups all wanted photographs. In addition, individuals and families wanted portraits. These were good years for photographers, and Gaynella and VanDerZee prospered. Within a year of the studio's opening, Gaynella's husband died, and shortly after that, Kate granted VanDerZee a divorce, making it possible for them to marry. At the studio Gaynella worked as receptionist and business manager. Eventually she learned to operate the cameras and, on occasion, actually took the photographs. However, she did only a small fraction of the studio work. The vast bulk of the portraits were made by VanDerZee.

The United States entered World War I in March 1917 and the Guarantee Photo Studio profited from the nation's military buildup. The young men of Harlem who volunteered for military service came to the studio for portraits before departing for Europe. The quality of these portraits proved to be the best advertisement VanDerZee could have hoped for. Family members and loved ones, who had been the recipients of the soldiers' portraits, chose to go to VanDerZee when they had portraits made to send to the men at the front. VanDerZee explained: "The boys used to have their pictures made before they went over, and then their mothers and fathers and girlfriends would have their pictures made and send them to their boys."[32] Thirty-one at the war's outbreak, he never was called up for military duty, but he did work for a while in a munitions factory.

In February 1919, VanDerZee, Gaynella, and all of Harlem celebrated the war's end and the grand return of the men of the 369th Infantry Regiment, formerly the 15th Regiment of the New York National Guard. The soldiers were from Harlem and were members of America's most decorated fighting units. The regiment's march up Fifth Avenue and into Harlem that February morning was seen as much a victory march over racism in the United States as over the German enemy. Black men, despite controversy about their abilities as soldiers, had demonstrated great valor and courage under fire.

For many African Americans the heroes' return symbolized the beginning of a new era. While the decade after World War I has been variously characterized as the Jazz Age or the Roaring Twenties, in Harlem there was no uncertainty. It was the decade of the Harlem Renaissance, the age of the New Negro.[33] VanDerZee would flourish in this period and in the decade and a half that followed, firmly establishing himself as Harlem's preeminent studio photographer. There were others.[34] But for half a century he simply was the best.

The majority of the photographs that made VanDerZee famous and brought him to the attention of a later generation of Americans were made during the period from 1920 to 1945: portraits of families, fraternal organizations, women's clubs, school groups, funerary portraits, and Harlem street scenes. As the times changed, so did VanDerZee's aesthetic. This is particularly evident in the portraits. In photographs made between 1905 and the end of World War I (work from Lenox, Virginia, and the Toussaint Conservatory) the emphasis is on the sitter. The use of props is minimal. The portraits from the postwar period are remarkably different. Employing a variety of studio props and elaborate painted backdrops (his own compositions as well as stock items from photographic suppliers), VanDerZee posed

Victory parade of the 369th Regiment, 1919
Donna Mussenden VanDerZee

The 369th Infantry Regiment, also known as the Harlem Hellfighters, was under attack in France for 191 days during World War I and never retreated. For their heroism, 150 of the regiment's men received the Croix de Guerre from the French government. On February 17, 1919, cheered by a crowd of one million onlookers, the returning soldiers marched up Fifth Avenue from Union Square, proceeding through Harlem along Lenox Avenue to 145th Street.

his subjects in dramatic *tableaux vivants,* placing more emphasis on the setting than previously. The sitters mimic poses found in contemporary magazine images, especially in the publications devoted to fashion, cinema, and the new activity of celebrity watching. Before the war VanDerZee had concentrated on getting a straightforward rendering of an individual; the portraits after 1920 show his adoption of certain media-provoked images of male and female. They also demonstrate the willingness of Harlemites to assume such standardized poses. How universally the public subscribed to the media ideal is exhibited in the work of other studio photographers. VanDerZee's success, like that of his peers both in and outside Harlem, depended on the ability to realize the effect the client desired.

In addition to maintaining a variety of backdrops, a room of furniture, and ersatz architectural elements (columns, gates, and so forth), VanDerZee kept available a selection of fashionable clothes for both men and women. Whether dressed in one's own finery or in the habiliment provided by VanDerZee, in the studio the client was offered the opportunity to construct alternative realities to the social roles determined by the exigencies of class

Her Cigarette, date unknown
Donna Mussenden VanDerZee

To make this photograph, Van-
DerZee worked by hand on the
negative of the still-life to add
the smoke coming from the cigarette, and then printed it together with the man's portrait.
The pendant photograph was
called *His Pipe*.

and race. The photographer's studio had traditionally provided the con-
sumers of its products an environment where various social personae and
masks could be presented to the camera. To a great degree this remained the
impetus behind having a portrait made in a studio during the years of
VanDerZee's ascendancy. In the nineteenth century, popular theatrical
productions had provided the models. In the twentieth century, film and
magazines as well were the source for studio characterizations, and the
composition, the lighting, and the poses in VanDerZee's portraits of black
stage and screen stars like Hazel Scott, Bill Robinson, and Mamie Smith are
reiterated in the portraits of Harlem's uncelebrated citizens.[35] VanDerZee's
studio arrangements were tastefully apropos. The "villa garden" backdrop
was used when the desired effect was to create the feeling of the dwelling
space of aristocratic gentry. However, if the mood was meant to be more

romantic, the "villa garden" was replaced with "moon over water." Neither of these backdrops would do for family groups. In these instances the "Gothic window" was used as the rear wall of the pictorial space. The "fireplace" was a symbol of domestic warmth and security. Into these backgrounded settings Victorian chairs and Edwardian tables, vases filled with flowers, leather-bound books, a grand piano, and other paraphernalia were carefully placed. These rooms, fabricated in the studio, unsurprisingly were congruent with the real interiors of actual Harlem homes where Van-DerZee frequently had portrait assignments.

The negative and the print were treated with an equally imaginative manipulation. Eyes were brightened and any unbecoming marks of time erased. Wisps of smoke were drawn forth from languidly held cigarettes, and every smile showed perfectly formed teeth. VanDerZee stopped at nothing when retouching his negatives and prints to arrive at the definition of beauty and elegance he and his clients wanted. This willingness to view negatives and prints as a stage on the way to the final pictorial presentation extended beyond portraits of the living into the realm of the dead. VanDer-Zee combination-printed his mortuary portraits, at times using as many as three or four different negatives to make a print. Mortuary portraits had their roots in the era of the earliest daguerreotypes from the United States and abroad, and daguerreotypists frequently posed the dead subjects with cemetery statuary or surrounded them with bouquets of flowers. VanDer-Zee's mortuary portraits, in which he mixed images of praying angels, excerpts from biblical texts, and the deceased's body, are simultaneously archaic, like the daguerreotypes, and modern. The iconographical elements are drawn from late Victorian and Edwardian visual traditions, but the way he put the component parts together is strikingly similar to avant-garde photomontage designs of the 1920s.[36]

In order to remain a successful studio photographer, VanDerZee had to be conversant with the many ways the product could be made attractive to the consumer. This helps to explain his willingness to manipulate prints and negatives in the darkroom. When he worked on out-of-the-studio assignments, he had less reason to use retouching techniques and, beginning in the 1920s, VanDerZee undertook numerous commissions that can best be described as photojournalistic. Church conventions, interior shots of a variety of businesses, and school convocations comprised a significant portion of his professional activity. One of the most unusual and dramatic commissions he undertook was his work for Marcus Garvey and the United Negro Improvement Association (UNIA). VanDerZee photographed the activities of the UNIA in the spring and summer of 1924, particularly the fourth International Convention, which was held at the organization's Liberty Hall in Harlem in August, an assignment that produced several thousand prints and even a 1925 calendar. This was during the period of Garvey's greatest notoriety and the public tarnishing of his reputation by many of the same

LEFT:
Drugstore soda fountain, 1943
Amon Carter Museum, Fort
Worth, Texas

BELOW:
Marcus Garvey and other UNIA officials reviewing a parade, 1924
Donna Mussenden VanDerZee

Wedding portrait, 1924
Donna Mussenden VanDerZee

Harlem intellectuals who had embraced him three years earlier. Garvey
wanted to blanket the black media with images of a vibrant and active
UNIA under his own careful stewardship. He hired VanDerZee. The bulk of
VanDerZee's work provides an unposed, candid journal of the activities of
the Garveyites. VanDerZee proved himself to be as good a reporter as he was
an imaginative artist. Parades, rallies, and the military drill of the Africa
Legion are some aspects of the encyclopedic record he put together for
Garvey. There are also some formal studio studies of UNIA families, and
these are posed as carefully as are all VanDerZee's portraits of this period.
The overall intention of the UNIA work was to evoke a mood of stability and
order. There were no intimations in the photographs of Garvey's impending
further fall from grace with the Harlem intelligentsia or his eventual im-
prisonment in a federal penitentiary.[37]

The work with Garvey was a highlight in a series of successes VanDerZee
enjoyed during the 1920s. He continued to attract Harlem celebrities to his
studio and was even more sought after by the community's thriving organizations and businesses. His portrait-studio business, especially the wedding

portrait commissions, flourished as well. He and Gaynella were financially comfortable and enjoyed the rewards of their economic success. Surviving leaves from their own family snapshot album contain pictures of beach parties and automobile excursions with friends. In the album there are also photographs of Lenox where, in place of Kate, Gaynella stands beside the aunts. Also among their personal portraits from these years is an image, taken by an anonymous friend, celebrating Gaynella's and VanDerZee's domestic felicity. The two of them stand in their dining room surrounded by the rewards of their labor. On the walls above the table, which is covered with food and beverages, they have secured tiers of his own photographs and other pictures. Gaynella holds one of her several cats. VanDerZee, who stands slightly behind her, looks on. There is a relaxed and almost wistful look on his face. His half-century of life would have taught him by now to acknowledge gain and to accept loss. By the time this photograph was made, Rachel was dead. She had died of peritonitis while on vacation in Maine in 1927. His mother had died in 1931. The one constant in his life at the time of this photograph (circa 1935) was the marriage the photograph celebrates.

James and Gaynella VanDerZee,
circa 1935
The Metropolitan Museum of Art, New York; gift of the James VanDerZee Institute, 1970 (1970.539.14)

V

The Great Depression struck Harlem hard. Like other Harlemites, the VanDerZees were forced to practice frugality, but the business was one of several that never failed.[38] They moved their studio to a former Chrysler automobile showroom at 2065 Seventh Avenue in 1930, and when they had to leave this space in the late 1930s, they went up the street to 2077 Seventh Avenue. The cataloguing of VanDerZee's work that was done in the 1980s demonstrates that during the worst years of economic downturn his volume of business decreased only slightly. Some people in Harlem continued to make money and to spend it, as attested by the lavish wedding parties VanDerZee photographed in the depression years. During the 1930s he and Gaynella also branched out into other business ventures, which were primarily under her direction. One of the more successful undertakings was the subletting of rooms in the houses they rented. She eventually advertised the room-rental service in newspapers with large circulation in the black community. For a while she also operated a gardening service.[39] VanDerZee had little or no involvement in these enterprises and, in consequence, was able to devote his attention to the photography studio. As a craftsman he was now at the apogee of his skills. When considered as a body, the prints from this period are consistently the most carefully made. These prints show how completely VanDerZee had mastered the various techniques he employed. What have not changed are the settings and compositions. In consequence, the images made in the 1930s differ but slightly from those executed in the preceding decade. In the post–World War I era VanDerZee developed a studio style that was uniquely his own. Henceforth, his photographs would have their own characteristic aspect that would continue well into the years after the next great war.

To get an insight into VanDerZee's difficult position as an American photographer at this time, we can turn to Cecil Beaton's 1938 book *Cecil Beaton's New York*. Beaton, already well on the way to establishing his reputation as one of Great Britain's leading photographers, intended the book to be part personal memoir, part travel guide, and an analysis of contemporary American customs. He illustrated the book with drawings, photographs of his own, and the works of other photographers. Several pages of one chapter were devoted to Harlem. That section, unfortunately, was boorishly racist, but in it Beaton featured a vignette that he entitled "the Harlem photographer." The photographer was James VanDerZee. A full-page portrait of VanDerZee (by Beaton) was included, along with a selection of VanDerZee's wedding and funerary portraits. Inexplicably, while Beaton acknowledged all of his other picture sources, he did not name VanDerZee in the text, nor did he include him in the listing of picture credits, which must have pained VanDerZee deeply. What payment or arrangements Beaton made with VanDerZee can only be surmised since Van-

DerZee never mentioned the Beaton episode in his autobiographical recountings. To his credit, although he was limited by a peculiarly provincial and xenophobic attitude toward black life, Beaton did discern the integral connection of VanDerZee's work with an attempt, even a misguided one like his own, to understand Harlem.[40]

As Gaynella's various entrepreneurial undertakings and the continued viability of the photography studio earned the VanDerZees a modest but comfortable living in even the worst years of the depression, they were well situated to take advantage of the slightly improving economy resulting from the legislative initiatives of Franklin Delano Roosevelt's first term. As real prosperity returned with the industrial buildup after the country's entry into the Second World War, the VanDerZees' prospects appeared even brighter. In March 1943 they rented a twelve-room house at 272 Lenox Avenue. The large number of rooms allowed them to continue letting space to long-term boarders and vacationing visitors, while the street-level storefront was converted into a display room, a posing chamber, and a darkroom. On August 3, 1945, two and one half months after V-E Day and three days before the first atomic bomb was dropped on Hiroshima, the 272 Lenox Avenue Corporation purchased the property at 272 Lenox Avenue.[41] The corporation's officers were Gaynella VanDerZee, president, and James VanDerZee, vice president. The purchase of the property they had been renting was a clear sign of their self-confidence and optimism. Although there had been a noticeable decline in some aspects of the portrait business during the war years, VanDerZee was certain the coming peace would boost the diminishing number of clients back to prewar levels. To a large degree, the waning of the portrait work was balanced by other commissions. In the 1930s he had begun making photographs of autopsies and other subjects related to insurance claims. He continued to accept both kinds of assignments after the war and began a lucrative business making identification photographs for taxicab drivers, security guards, and small tradesmen. Although he and Gaynella were both in their fifties when they took over the mortgage on 272 Lenox (he was fifty-nine and she was fifty-four), the combined income from the patchwork quilt of business enterprises represented by the 272 Lenox Avenue Corporation was good. They were earning more money now than at any time before. But this moment of their greatest financial expansion also harbored the seeds of their contracting prospects. Some signs of the fate of the studio might have been discernible in 1945, but VanDerZee was swept up with the rest of the nation by the euphoria of the nearing end of another war. The last war had been the catalyst of his career. He had every reason to believe this second war would have a similar effect.

Instead, every aspect of his formal portrait business declined after the Second World War. When he was later asked to explain the demise of his portrait business, VanDerZee would place blame on the trend toward the informal snapshots that most of his customers desired and their ability to

Page from *Cecil Beaton's New York* (1938) featuring his photograph of VanDerZee

Front office, VanDerZee's studio at 2065 Seventh Avenue, 1932
Donna Mussenden VanDerZee

Interior of VanDerZee's studio at 2065 Seventh Avenue, circa 1937
Amon Carter Museum, Fort Worth, Texas

make such photographs themselves.[42] While some of the losses could be attributed to the increasing use of easy-to-operate roll-film cameras and a growing public interest in amateur photography, that is only a part of the explanation. Portraits VanDerZee made in the early and middle years of the 1940s offer an added insight into his decline. The photographs clearly illustrate how captivated VanDerZee was by the pictorial conventions he had started using twenty-five years earlier. The painted backdrops, the architectural details, and the glamorous poses that made a VanDerZee photograph a prized possession to the preceding generation now marked the photographer's images as quaint relics from another era. VanDerZee did not change his style, nor did he come up with a more appropriate aesthetic. The results are sometimes jarring as the contemporary sitters attempt to appear comfortable in the Victorian-Edwardian settings. But there they are, women in leotards and men in leisure suits cloistered in the brooding silence of the "Gothic window" backdrop and judiciously avoiding contact with the chipped classical column. For a while, in the late 1940s, VanDerZee even

GGG Photo, 272 Lenox Avenue,
circa 1943
Donna Mussenden VanDerZee

VanDerZee stopped using the name Guarantee Photo Studio when a lawyer told him that the name "Guarantee" was reserved for banks and trust companies. He changed it to GGG in an eccentric tribute to his wife, Gaynella Greenlee.

Advertisement for photo restoration, circa 1942
Donna Mussenden VanDerZee

He tried me on the sofa,
He tried me on the chair,
He tried me on the window sill,
But he couldnt get it there;
He tried me lying on the couch,
I stood against the wall,
I even sat upon the floor,
It wouldnt work at all;
He tried it this and that way,
Oh! how I did laugh,
To see how many ways he tried
To take my photograph.

He Tried Me, 1935
Donna Mussenden VanDerZee

This photograph was probably taken for a calendar.

devised a printing system in which he would photograph the sitter against an unpainted backdrop and then, using a negative that held the image of a setting, make a combination print that united the subject with the "room." The history of studio photography clearly shows that the profession did not end with the wide distribution of easy-to-use cameras and dependable color film. Studio photographers still flourished, although in fewer numbers, just as they had at the turn of the century when VanDerZee was getting started. People in Harlem continued to go to studio photographers for certain kinds of photographs. But eventually they stopped going to VanDerZee.

The Harlem VanDerZee worked in during the 1940s and the 1950s was undergoing radical changes itself. When VanDerZee and Kate first moved there in 1908, Harlem was a place of middle-class aspirations and had the bright aspect that newly built neighborhoods always have. Of course, in the fullest sense of the word it was not really a neighborhood yet. Harlem became a neighborhood when it had the full mix of professionals, services, and the variety of life experiences and human types a thriving urban district should possess. This was the Harlem VanDerZee and Gaynella saw take shape just before World War I and then flourish in the 1920s. Harlem came through the Great Depression bruised but essentially healthy. Then, like the rest of New York, Harlem had a surge of economic and cultural growth in the years immediately preceding and after World War II. This continued into the 1950s but in tandem with another, more disquieting phenomenon. The black middle class was abandoning Harlem. Most moved to the suburban districts of Queens, the Bronx, and Brooklyn, while very successful upper-middle-class professionals chose Westchester County and Long Island. This migration out of economically and socially mixed black neighborhoods had a devastating impact on the future of black metropolitan districts in every part of the country, for it resulted in the creation of unhealthy ghettos in place of viable communities.

As a photographer, merchant, and property owner, VanDerZee was intimately connected to Harlem through the web of relationships he and Gaynella had made over the four decades of their lives there. His business had almost entirely been based on commerce within the community. When the majority of potential and actual customers began to drift away to other parts of the metropolitan region, the businesses they left behind, like VanDerZee's, were doomed in most cases to failure. In retrospect, no single agent can be identified as the cause of the dismal economic record of the photography studio or other ventures operated by the 272 Lenox Avenue Corporation in the decades after World War II. Rather, a congeries of factors has to be taken into account. The failure of the community to sustain a healthy local economy is certainly significant.[43] So, too, are the changing tastes of the popular audience. Finally, there is the issue of the VanDerZees' advancing age. At a time in life when most men and women consider reducing their activity, they had to demand more of themselves.

VI

Every morning except Sunday, VanDerZee opened the studio. Most days his only visitors were neighborhood children inquiring whether they were needed to run any errands. Sometimes he asked to have something taken to the post office or a sandwich brought to him from a nearby restaurant. Mostly, he sat in the front room of the studio, watched the pedestrian traffic pass by, and waited for clients who never came. He also waited to see what Judge Stoute would do. Another year had passed, and although he and Gaynella had yet to pay anything, Stoute had let them stay on. In December 1967, when they were more than two years behind in payments to Stoute, a ray of hope penetrated the gloom of the studio on Lenox Avenue. A young photographer who was researching material for a forthcoming exhibition on Harlem history at the Metropolitan Museum of Art had unexpectedly come across VanDerZee's studio. His name was Reginald McGhee. He told VanDerZee that he was particularly interested in photographs of Harlem between the wars. Did VanDerZee have anything he might like to show him, McGhee inquired? VanDerZee, who had saved just about every negative he ever exposed, led McGhee to a rear storage room and showed him the hundreds of boxes and shopping bags filled with prints and negatives. Several hours later, as he walked down Lenox Avenue with a box of VanDerZee's photographs, McGhee realized he held the nucleus of the Metropolitan exhibition. It was like stumbling across a "gold mine," he would later say.[46] The next day McGhee shared his discovery of VanDerZee with Allon Schoener.

The exhibition McGhee was working on was to be called "Harlem On My Mind." The title for the exhibition had come from a song lyric in Irving Berlin's musical "A Thousand Cheers." The title had been selected by Allon Schoener, who had also conceived the idea for the exhibition. In 1966, as visual arts director for the New York State Council on the Arts, he had organized the successful exhibition "Portals of the Past" at the Jewish Museum. In the summer of 1967 Schoener met with Thomas P. Hoving, who only recently had been appointed director of the Metropolitan Museum of Art and was looking for innovative ideas for shows. He proposed an exhibition similar to "Portals of the Past," which would focus on the black experience in New York. As with the exhibition at the Jewish Museum, Schoener wanted to use a multimedia format, including slides, audio, film, and mural-size blowups of photographs.[47] In November, at a press conference at the Schomburg Collection, housed in the West 135th Street Branch of the New York Public Library next door to the building where VanDerZee had opened his first studio in 1917, Hoving announced the plans for an exhibition, to open in October 1968, that, he said, would be a "study of [Harlem's] achievements and contribution to American life and [New York City]."[48] Hoving introduced Schoener, who would be the director of the

Exhibition Committee. Schoener then introduced the man he had chosen to be the exhibition's director of photographic research, Reginald McGhee. Schoener knew McGhee from the Council on the Arts and had asked him to join the Metropolitan Exhibition Committee. The introductions of Schoener and McGhee to the public came three weeks before McGhee met VanDerZee.

McGhee found VanDerZee's studio around the time of the Exhibition Committee's first meeting, December 6. Within a week he mailed VanDerZee a check for one hundred dollars, a retainer for the seventy-nine prints VanDerZee had let him take. McGhee wrote that the number of prints the Exhibition Committee selected would determine the size of the fee the museum would offer VanDerZee. VanDerZee received the letter shortly before Christmas, just in time to buy gifts for Gaynella and have the kind of Christmas dinner they had not expected to enjoy.[49] VanDerZee also contacted Judge Stoute. He told Stoute about the letter and held forth another promise of swift payment of debt. Stoute agreed to wait an unspecified amount of time before he would press on with selling the building. After New Year's Day VanDerZee began to telephone McGhee and inquire about the money. McGhee gave him Schoener's number. As the winter wore on, VanDerZee called both men regularly. The answer was always the same; neither could tell him how many of his pictures were going to be used, and neither knew how desperately VanDerZee needed money.[50] Over time, Van-DerZee's situation became clearer to them, but they were not in a position to advance him money.

In April, McGhee gave VanDerZee a preliminary figure: two thousand dollars. The figure had been arrived at after Schoener and McGhee agreed that living photographers would be paid in accordance with rates set by the American Society for Magazine Photographers. However, they were still in the selection process. They also were becoming involved in a heated political debate. Harlem artists decried Schoener's idea of a multimedia exhibition that featured photographs. The artists wanted a more traditional approach. Romare Bearden wrote Schoener in May and suggested that either he "phase the show out . . . or else start immediately to work in the interests of the kind of show the community as a whole would want."[51] The disagreement between the Metropolitan Exhibition Committee and the Harlem artists slowed everything. In July, Schoener and McGhee agreed that they would not be able to open the exhibition in October and pushed the opening date back to January 1969. While attempting to defuse the controversy about the nature of the show, they continued to work on the selection of materials and develop the exhibition catalogue. All VanDerZee could do was wait.

In September an Exhibition Committee staff member, Louise Broecker, made the final selection. She had visited VanDerZee at his studio and had asked to see if there might be additional items of interest in his collection. VanDerZee suggested she look at his negatives. Broecker recalls that there were thousands of glass and celluloid negatives. She selected several dozen and asked to have new prints from them. When the rest of the staff saw the new images, they agreed with Broecker that they should be included in the exhibition. After the inclusion of these photographs, McGhee labeled Van-DerZee the "single largest contributor" to the show.[52] In late September, the museum mailed a check for three thousand five hundred dollars to VanDer-Zee, a little less than half of what was owed to Stoute. As far as Stoute was concerned, it was not enough, and he kept the house on the market. The opening of "Harlem On My Mind" was three months away, but even now a storm of controversy was beginning to erupt.

All summer and into the autumn, the Harlem artists and the museum Exhibition Committee continued to meet in an attempt to resolve the conflicting ideas about the content of the coming exhibition. But in November the dialogue was broken off when the Harlem Cultural Council notified Hoving that its members were withdrawing endorsement of "Harlem On My Mind."[53] After Thanksgiving Romare Bearden and another black painter, Benny Andrews, met with Jean Hutson, the director of the Schomburg Center, to discuss plans to picket the museum when the exhibition opened in January.[54] Trouble was looming on another horizon for Hoving and the Exhibition Committee as well. There were people who were disturbed about what they heard the exhibition catalogue might contain.

Allon Schoener was planning a book to accompany the exhibition that would be a collection of newspaper and magazine articles reflecting events and trends in Harlem's history. He characterized the book as an "extension" of "Harlem On My Mind," intended to present the reader "with a selective barrage of information, transferring into book form the structure, technique, and emotional impact of a multi-media exhibition." Schoener also wanted to include an essay written by a Harlem resident, "an ordinary citizen, a true representative of the people." In August, at McGhee's urging, he read a high-school term paper written by a summer intern at the New York Council on the Arts, Candice VanEllison. Schoener liked it but thought it was too "academic" and suggested to VanEllison that she edit out the footnotes and recast the quotations so that a reader would assume the essay was entirely written in her own words. VanEllison, by now a college student at the University of Bridgeport, was excited at the prospects of being published and agreed to make the changes Schoener requested.[55]

In a section of her essay entitled "Intergroup Relations," VanEllison had written about black Harlemites' relations with three other New York ethnic groups: Irish, Puerto Ricans, and Jews. What she said about Jewish/African American relations would lead to controversy. Discussing the black migration after World War I to northeastern cities, she wrote:

> Anti-Jewish feeling is a natural result of the Black Northern Migration. Afro-Americans in Northeastern industrial cities are constantly coming in contact with Jews. Pouring into lower-income areas in the city, the Afro-American invariably pushes out the Jew.

> Behind every hurdle that the Afro-American has yet to jump stands
> the Jew who has already cleared it.

VanEllison concluded her discussion of Jewish/African American relations
with the following statement: "Blacks may find that anti-Jewish sentiments
place them, for once, within a majority. Thus our contempt for the Jew
makes us feel more completely American in sharing a national prejudice."[56]
These two passages raised the ire of many white (Jewish and non-Jewish)
New Yorkers. The contents of the essay were divulged by unidentified
parties before the book reached the public, and it was immediately branded
anti-Semitic. Pressure was put on Mayor John V. Lindsay, a close friend of
Hoving, to demand that the museum not publish the offending remarks, and
on January 15 he asked that the introduction be withdrawn, since it was
"racist and mainly anti-Semitic."[57] It is not clear whether Lindsay had yet
had an opportunity to read the introduction; he certainly had not read
VanEllison's research paper. If he had, the mayor might have been surprised
to discover that VanEllison's words, cited in her high-school term paper,
were taken from a highly regarded study on ethnicity in America. She had
used *Beyond the Melting Pot* by Nathan Glazer and Daniel Moynihan.
Glazer would later say it was "ironic" that the essay was attacked as being
anti-Semitic when parts of it were "quoted from a book which is clearly
not."[58] Glazer, however, was interviewed after the exhibition's opening, and
prior to his comment no one except Schoener and McGhee knew about
VanEllison's sources. In consequence, attacks on VanEllison and Hoving as
anti-Semites continued unabated. Word was leaked to the press that the
Jewish Defense League planned to picket the museum when the exhibition
opened.

VanDerZee, of course, was not a target of the rancor. Although "Harlem
On My Mind" was to be the most influential event in his professional life,
VanDerZee's direct participation was slight. As late as the middle of January, he was still unknown to everyone except the members of the Exhibition
Committee. After he had learned from Stoute that the money he had earned
from the exhibition would not be enough to forestall the sale of the property,
he became preoccupied with his own problems. Gaynella's response to the
sign that her husband's achievements were about to be recognized remains
shrouded in mystery. No one but VanDerZee had seen her in almost a year.
McGhee had spoken with her once on the telephone, shortly after he had
mailed the retainer of one hundred dollars, when she called to tell him that
she was VanDerZee's business manager and that all monetary affairs had to
be transacted with her. Whenever he visited the studio, McGhee says, Gaynella and VanDerZee communicated with an elaborate system of tapping,
she from the floor above and he on the studio ceiling.[59] Gaynella's withdrawal
from society was an ominous sign of the emotional problems that would
haunt her remaining years. Both she and VanDerZee understood the fair-

newspaper, may have been correct in its assessment that once it became public knowledge that a Jew, Allon Schoener, had been the editor of what was actually an evenly balanced research essay and that it was not a black writer's anti-Semitic diatribe, the controversy would subside.[64] Three days after the publication of Schoener's interview, the Jewish Defense League ended its protest. That left only the Black Emergency Cultural Coalition. Although their numbers had declined since their appearance on the museum steps on opening night, the black artists were still vocal in their demand that the Metropolitan put on an exhibition of African American art. On February 18, Hoving announced that the museum was indeed planning on a show that would survey the work of black artists from 1876 to 1969. While he was vague about the date, Hoving promised it would be within the year.[65] With this announcement the last group of protesters departed, and although its merits and weaknesses would be debated for months to come, "Harlem On My Mind" finally was no longer considered only in terms of contending political forces.

Given the controversy, it is not surprising that the exhibition drew large

Bridesmaids in Harlem, date unknown
The Studio Museum in Harlem Archives, James VanDerZee Photographic Collection; and the Donna VanDerZee Collection

crowds. During the first week and a half it was open, over seventy-seven thousand visitors saw "Harlem On My Mind." Every day that the museum was open, long lines of museum-goers of all races stretched down Fifth Avenue, waiting for an opportunity to see the exhibition everyone was talking about. VanDerZee's photographs continued to be applauded. When the *New York Post* ran an illustrated article covering the exhibition, half of the reproduced photographs were his.[66] VanDerZee saw the exhibition only on the one occasion when Reginald McGhee brought him to the opening. Gaynella never saw it. Both she and VanDerZee remained closeted in their Harlem brownstone.

"Harlem On My Mind" closed on April 6. Reginald McGhee and Allon Schoener were preparing to return to the New York State Council on the Arts, and Thomas Hoving had already arranged to rid himself and the Metropolitan of the artifacts that had been a part of the exhibition. (Later, in 1970, the VanDerZee Institute made a gift of VanDerZee prints to the Metropolitan Museum of Art.) The few items that belonged to private lenders or that had been borrowed from other institutions were to be returned, but the photo murals were consigned to the trash. Although Jean Hutson and Hoving were not on the friendliest terms, she was still able to convince him that it would be a better idea to let her take the murals back to the Schomburg Center rather than to have them destroyed. Hoving relented, and Hutson hired a truck and brought all but two back to her library. They remain part of the Schomburg's permanent collection.[67]

In late March, two weeks before the exhibition closed, VanDerZee called Schoener. He explained that he and Gaynella were about to be evicted from their home and asked Schoener to intercede on their behalf. Schoener was especially struck by the urgency in VanDerZee's voice and arranged to put him in touch with Howard Squadron, the Council on the Arts' lawyer. All Squadron could do was to report back that the eviction proceedings were entirely legal and could not be prevented. Shortly after getting this information, VanDerZee contacted McGhee. He wanted McGhee to rescue the collection of negatives and prints if they had to leave quickly. McGhee agreed, and he told VanDerZee to call him when the time arrived. VanDerZee telephoned Schoener every night during his last week in the house. He wept, Schoener recalled, each time the topic of the house came up.[68] On Saturday, April 5, the forlorn VanDerZee called McGhee and requested that he come over the next day to start moving out the prints and negatives. That Sunday McGhee made several trips between his Brooklyn apartment and the Lenox Avenue house, but by the end of the day he had only begun to make a dent into the stacks of boxes. He told VanDerZee he would be back the next morning, the day of the actual eviction.[69]

On Monday, April 7, the day after "Harlem On My Mind" closed, VanDerZee and Gaynella were evicted, an event that was covered by the *New York Times*.[70] He took a photograph of the remnants of their fifty years together now packed into the crudely stacked boxes on the sidewalk. All but two of the cats Gaynella had so dearly loved fled in terror as the city-hired movers went from room to room. The cats disappeared into the streets of Harlem and were never found. A distraught Gaynella had to be restrained when she attacked the City Marshal with a can of insect spray. Ultimately she was forced into an ambulance, sedated, and taken to the hospital.[71] VanDerZee registered into a hotel in the South Bronx, taking with him as many of his prints as he could carry in shopping bags. The boxes of belongings and all the furniture were dispatched to a warehouse. McGhee had rescued many of the prints and negatives, as VanDerZee had requested, and moved them into temporary storage in his Brooklyn apartment.

VII

VanDerZee had made more than three thousand dollars from his association with "Harlem On My Mind" for the onetime use of his photographs, and this had led him to believe that they would eventually make him a wealthy man. For the first time in years, he no longer felt powerless.

In June 1969 an agreement was signed establishing the James VanDerZee Institute. Its chief officers were: Chairman, James VanDerZee; Project Director, Reginald McGhee; and Administrative Director, Charles Innis, who was also director of the Studio Museum in Harlem. During its lifetime the institute sponsored scores of shows around the United States in which the work of new black photographers was featured. Ironically, the lure for visitors to each exhibition was VanDerZee's work of forty and fifty years before. At each institute exhibition VanDerZee's photographs were introduced to a new audience. The first major show the institute put on was at the Public Library in Lenox, Massachusetts, in the summer of 1970. VanDerZee had come home again, although he did not visit Lenox himself. The Lenox show was enthusiastically received, and the institute went on to arrange eleven additional exhibitions between 1970 and 1972. There also was publishing activity. In 1969 *The World of James VanDerZee* was published, followed in 1973 by *James VanDerZee*.[72] In both books large numbers of VanDerZee photographs were reproduced. The shows and the books forced critics to ponder VanDerZee's place in photography's history.

Although he was not oblivious to the activity swirling about him, VanDerZee let McGhee manage his affairs while he attempted to take care of an ailing Gaynella. She would remain an invalid until her death in 1976. Her mental and physical state deteriorated over the seven years she and VanDerZee shared the small apartment on West 94th Street where Welfare Department officials moved them. Visitors often heard her demand of her husband that he "take me home." When they were first evicted, VanDerZee still clung to the hope that he could regain his lost property. He did not believe that the mortgage holder, Herman Stoute, had given up on any chance of a workable relationship with him and Gaynella, even after Stoute had sold the building.

According to his calculations, the VanDerZee Institute would earn him enough money within six months to a year to buy back the house on Lenox Avenue. In this hope, he was to be seriously disappointed: during its first year the institute paid him only a few hundred dollars. McGhee had never intended that the institute would act as a benefacting agent for VanDerZee. For McGhee, the institute was created to showcase the current generation of African American photographers (of which McGhee was one) and to demonstrate his personal organizational and curatorial talents.[73] These dramatically different conceptions of the purpose of the institute would lead to a complete break between McGhee and VanDerZee eight years later.

During the first half of the 1970s VanDerZee became something of a celebrity. He was featured on the Public Broadcasting System's programs "Tony Brown's Black Journal" and the "Dick Cavett Show"; he was regularly written about in America and Europe; and he was the subject of a film. However, his hope of financial salvation continued to be disappointed. In 1975 a limited-edition portfolio of VanDerZee prints was authorized for sale to private collectors and institutions, but the profits went to the institute. In fact, VanDerZee's association with the institute earned him almost no income. VanDerZee was embittered by the knowledge that the institute was being funded by various grants that provided salaries for its staff but not for him. He was angered even more when rumors circulated widely that hundreds of vintage prints, prints he had made in the first thirty years of his career, were being sold by the institute, something McGhee always denied. Shortly after he and Gaynella were moved into the apartment on 94th Street, VanDerZee had begun selling the prints he had kept for himself. By 1973 he was offering prints for two and three hundred dollars. Other than the small income from such a sale now and then, he relied on welfare payments and Social Security benefits. VanDerZee blamed McGhee for his poverty and wanted now to revoke the agreement that had established the institute.

If the institute was a financial disappointment, its benefits were entirely unexpected. A variety of people were attracted to VanDerZee the person because of the publicity he received, and he made himself available to all visitors to his cramped apartment. Many were curiosity seekers who didn't return after the first visit; others came at every opportunity. They became his dearest friends and most ardent advocates.

Among them was Ruth Sherman, who had been active in Harlem cultural affairs for years and had been impressed with VanDerZee's photographs since seeing them in "Harlem On My Mind." They did not meet, however, until 1975, when she visited the VanDerZees to have him sign her copy of *The World of James VanDerZee* and was appalled when she saw the squalid living conditions in the apartment. VanDerZee talked freely with her about his plight and what he now construed to be the unfair treatment he was suffering at the hands of McGhee. He was in danger, he told her, of losing the possessions that had been in storage since the eviction because of past-due storage payments. Sherman, who says she considered the aged photographer a "national treasure," immediately set out to aid him.[74] Although she attempted to convince McGhee that the institute had an obligation to care for its chairman's needs, Sherman directed her energy at enlisting succor from people she personally knew. In the spring of 1975 she organized a group and named it the "Friends of VanDerZee." Shortly afterward she hosted a benefit for the VanDerZees. The money garnered from this event, eight hundred dollars, was applied to the storage bill. She also assisted VanDerZee, as best she could, in his attempt to wrest back control of his photographs and negatives from the institute.

The relationship between VanDerZee and McGhee remained cordial, but their original warm friendship had cooled significantly. After the emergence of the Friends as an organized support group, McGhee became a diminishing presence and influence in VanDerZee's life. Meanwhile, another of the Friends, Camille Billops, arranged for VanDerZee to return to active photography after a seven-year hiatus. In the store of a friend in SoHo, Billops held what she called an "Event." People came from all over to see VanDerZee, who was quickly becoming a legend in New York. The affair lasted several hours. VanDerZee made a series of portraits in a part of the store that had been set up with lights and a few props, photographing Billops and her husband James Hatch, Sara Penn, the proprietor of the store, Vivian Brown, and Benny Andrews. VanDerZee had become friends, through Billops, with Mary Ellen Andrews, who was then married to Benny Andrews. Andrews, the foe of "Harlem On My Mind" in 1969, now found himself posing in front of VanDerZee's camera and enjoying every minute of it. The sitters paid VanDerZee fifty dollars for the privilege.[75]

During the spring of 1976 VanDerZee began collaborating with Billops on a book of his funeral photographs. One day early in May, she was met at the front door by the neighbor who lived across the hall from the VanDerZees. Gaynella had fallen and broken her hip. Billops helped to get her to a hospital.[76] VanDerZee moved with difficulty now, but he went to the hospital whenever he could until Gaynella's death on June 29. She was eighty-four when she died, three days after her husband's ninetieth birthday. The birthday celebration had been planned for July 1. Several of VanDerZee's closest friends of the last seven years came, and he turned the occasion into a wake for Gaynella. The next day he went to view the body at the funeral parlor, but decided against going to the services, asking another photographer to make the casket portrait. Only a handful of people attended the funeral. Among the mourners was McGhee. VanDerZee did not discover McGhee had been at the funeral until years later.[77]

Eventually, as the shock of Gaynella's death eased, VanDerZee adapted to

Benny Andrews, 1976
Donna Mussenden VanDerZee

Artist Benny Andrews (b. 1930)
teaches at Queens College in New
York City. His work has been
widely exhibited.

his life as a widower. His stream of visitors continued, and he resumed
working with Camille Billops on the book of funeral portraits. The project
eventually became *The Harlem Book of the Dead*.[78] VanDerZee also began
to travel. He was invited to Philadelphia to receive a "visiting artist" award
and to Seton Hall University in New Jersey to receive an Honorary Doctor
of Law degree. Although VanDerZee wrote to a friend that he particularly
missed Gaynella on holidays, he did not let the death of his spouse mark the
end of his own renewed activity. In 1977 he helped work on a film about his
career and made more jaunts away from New York. In October of that year
a one-man show of recently made prints at the Alternative Center for
International Art in New York brought renewed attention from the critics.
Although the negatives came from the institute, it was not involved in
planning the exhibition.[79] Since 1969 the institute had been the moving force
behind major exhibitions of VanDerZee's photographs. This show signaled
the end of an era: henceforth there were to be no more VanDerZee Institute
exhibitions.

After eight years of existence, the VanDerZee Institute found itself financially unable to support itself and to properly care for its collections. In
addition, in 1977 the institute had to move out of its offices at the Metropolitan Museum of Art. That year Reginald McGhee, representing the institute,
approached Courtney Callendar, then the director of the Studio Museum in
Harlem, with a proposal to merge the institute and the museum. The mu-

seum resisted a merger, but agreed to accept the VanDerZee collection, in keeping with its mission to collect, preserve, exhibit, and interpret art of the African Diaspora. The transfer of the institute's principal assets was made in compliance with the New York State Attorney General's office, which monitors non-profit organizations. Although both the Metropolitan Museum of Art and the Schomburg Library had previously accepted gifts of VanDerZee prints from the institute, the overwhelming majority of the prints and negatives were transferred to the Studio Museum on July 1, 1978. Shortly afterward, McGhee left New York to live in Atlanta.

In August 1977 VanDerZee told an interviewer he was considering "looking for a wife before I become too old to marry again."[80] The woman he married in June 1978 was Donna Mussenden, the young companion who had accompanied him on his recent ventures beyond New York City. A graduate of Howard University, where she had studied sociology, Donna was the director of Gallery 62 on East 52nd Street in New York City when she first sought out VanDerZee after seeing one of his books. Now, although he had numerous friends and was receiving many callers who were interested in his life work, there was still the void in his life left by Gaynella's death. Like Gaynella, and in contrast to Kate, Donna recognized and encouraged his genius. She also took care of the man, seeing that VanDerZee got some long overdue medical care.[81] In late 1979, almost a year and a half after their wedding, VanDerZee left the small apartment he had been living in and took up residence in the more spacious penthouse on upper Broadway that Donna found for them. Regenia Perry, who had met VanDerZee in 1969 and had written the introduction for the 1973 monograph of his work, said that his marriage to Donna was a "godsend," and that because of her, VanDerZee was "rejuvenated."[82]

VanDerZee's reputation continued to flourish. Donna organized exhibitions in the Midwest and on the West Coast, made all the travel arrangements, and got him to each engagement safely. During these years the award ceremonies and the speaking engagements nearly doubled. Also, with Donna's help, he returned to portrait photography. His first client was one of America's most famous and beloved film and television personalities, Bill Cosby, whose idea it was to be photographed by VanDerZee. Furniture and studio props were taken out of storage, dusted off, spruced up, and readied for use, and a stage designer was hired to re-create VanDerZee's backdrops. Over the next three years, VanDerZee made portraits of some of the country's more famous African American celebrities. Among them were Miles Davis, Cicely Tyson, Eubie Blake, Muhammad Ali, and Romare Bearden. Bearden, who had opposed "Harlem On My Mind" in 1969 before he had ever seen a VanDerZee photograph, now was one of VanDerZee's most vocal admirers. In Bearden's and the other photographs, VanDerZee turned back the clock and worked at recreating the look of the portraits he had made in the 1920s and 1930s. Although the fee VanDerZee demanded was consider-

Donna Mussenden VanDerZee,
1982
Donna Mussenden VanDerZee

able, the series of celebrity portraits proved to be a successful venture, for, as Regenia Perry pointed out, here was a "rare opportunity to be photographed by the most renowned of all Black American photographers."[83] The portrait of Perry, which VanDerZee made in February 1983, was the last of these sittings he would undertake.

While VanDerZee's initial feeling about the transfer of the institute's VanDerZee collection to the Studio Museum may have been positive, he had by late 1977 begun to express reservations to McGhee.[84] Soon the museum found itself caught in a burgeoning dispute between VanDerZee and the institute over ownership of the collection. In 1981 VanDerZee filed a legal suit against the museum for the return of the photographs and negatives, and two years later a distribution agreement was reached whereby the parties each received a representative portion of the collection: the estate was given 50 percent; the institute, now represented by James VanDerZee, 25 percent; and the museum, 25 percent.[85] With the aid of public and private grants, the museum has catalogued the prints and begun to catalogue the negatives in its VanDerZee collection, which is part of a new archive and research center. Images from the museum's collection have been included in scholarly publications and in exhibitions, among them "Harlem Renaissance: Art of Black America" of 1987.

VanDerZee had been dead a year when the settlement was reached. He died on May 15, 1983, in Howard University Hospital in Washington, D.C.,

Regenia Perry, 1983
Dr. Regenia A. Perry

where he had come to receive a Honorary Doctor of Humane Letters degree from Howard University. The day was sunny and midspring warm, but not muggy or hot. The exercises were long, but when the degree was conferred on him, he accepted it with the same gentlemanly decorum seen in all the films and videotape records his wife kept and spoken of by his many intimates. Late in the evening he began to have an irregular heartbeat and was rushed to the hospital. He died in his sleep shortly after midnight. He would have been ninety-six in five weeks, but as he had said about his mother when describing how she expired, he had "just [run] out of breath."[86]

VIII

James VanDerZee's place in the history of American photography appears secure. When his work was first gaining critical attention, he was alternately labeled a social documentarian and a "naif."[87] The person most responsible for his early fame, Reginald McGhee, stated that VanDerZee's name should be added to a list that included such prominent figures in photography as "Steichen, Stieglitz, Hine . . . Parks . . . and Lange."[88] Although he had seen only a fraction of VanDerZee's work at the time that he made his claim, McGhee obviously already believed VanDerZee was one of the more important photographers of the twentieth century. What went unanswered was just where to situate VanDerZee in such august company. Was VanDerZee a photojournalist like Gordon Parks, the only African American on the list? A pictorialist like the young Alfred Stieglitz? A social realist like Lewis Hine? And what did he have in common with Dorothea Lange, the only woman McGhee had included? Or with Edward Steichen? As a student of the history of photography, McGhee was certainly familiar with the work of these photographers, and he understood that the one certain thing they had in common with VanDerZee was that all were his contemporaries. Yet while they were well known, VanDerZee was just beginning to be recognized. And this, of course, was due to McGhee's own recent efforts. McGhee also realized that unless the photographs were brought into the growing discourse about photography, they would continue to be excluded from historical accounts. That was the great legacy of the James VanDerZee Institute; it brought James VanDerZee's almost century-long commitment to making photographs to the attention of the rest of us. It would be our obligation to understand the nature of the gift.

Once it was established that VanDerZee was not working in the modernist tradition being championed by some in the 1960s, it seemed relatively easy to exclude him from serious consideration, as Beaumont Newhall did. In his 1982 revision of *The History of Photography,* the founding curator of the Museum of Modern Art's photography department did not mention VanDerZee.[89] More recent scholarly work has challenged such attempts to establish any kind of photographic canon or the implied iconographic hierarchy that was subtly being erected. This more catholic view of the history of photography has assured the inclusion of photographers like James VanDerZee in the continuing, lively discussion about photography and the various modes of photographic expression.

That VanDerZee's work has been freed from invidious comparisons with that of his chronological contemporaries makes it easier to assess his achievement. Other studio photographers — some African American, some not — worked in Harlem during the years of VanDerZee's greatest success, but their work is consistently less compelling than his. How do VanDerZee's images differ from theirs, and in what way or ways are they similar? Why did he and other studio photographers employ the visual syntax first set forth in the 1860s? And in conjunction with that question, one might ask why twentieth-century clients found these archaic formulae so alluring? Finally, what, after all, is the relationship of VanDerZee's photographs to the social milieu in which they were made, and what can they divulge about the African American experience in the United States?

We can begin to answer these questions. Some critics have proposed that black Americans have wanted stylish images of themselves to counter prevailing racist stereotypes of African Americans in the wide variety of media aimed at reaching the country's white population.[90] According to this argument, the frightened sambos and grinning mammies of films and advertisements were symbolically supplanted by the elegant and self-assured men and women encountered in portraits like those made by VanDerZee. To whatever degree the oppressed internalize the oppressor's characterization of them, this theory of reactive self-imaging may well be accurate, but it is also extremely reductionist. Surely, the victims of oppression can make their own decisions and do arrive at awarenesses that are self-generated and not necessarily merely responses to their minority status or to racism.

Originally intended as gifts to intimates or for personal reflection, in their first use such photographs as VanDerZee took adorned fireplace mantelpieces in parlors and dressing tables and vanities in bedrooms. They did not acquire the status of museum art or publishable images until fifty years after they were made. Therefore, although later interpretations of the images are not to be discounted, their original meanings to their first viewers have to be taken into account whenever they come under critical analysis. The portraits proclaimed some essential truth about the sitters that they could assume the viewers would recognize. The re-created scenarios in front of the camera, in other words, would not have been alien to the subjects. That there was an authentic Edwardian black American experience comes as a surprise only if the history of African Americans has been obtained through sources where the theory of the black as helpless victim takes precedence over other aspects of black Americans' history. VanDerZee's clients wanted a testimony to their successes and achievements, a sign of their fully realized humanity. The photographer's creative use of the three-dimensional spaces framed by the camera, and his later treatment of the negative and finished print as analogous plastic surfaces, helped to accomplish the customer's goal. His artistry assured him continued success.

When Roland Barthes chose to use a VanDerZee photograph to help explicate his somewhat idiosyncratic theory of how a photograph engages the human mind, he was demonstrating that, as with other human-made objects, the "meaning" of these photographs is only limited by the boundaries of the imagination that encounters them. For Barthes a photograph is "good" when it inspires us, as we consider it, to reconsider ourselves, to stop the incessant interior dialogue and ponder the ways we are connected to everything and to each other.[91] In such moments the photograph becomes the conduit that delivers us again to the world and returns us to the wider community of humanity. Good photographs are full of wonder waiting to be discovered. They remind us in so many ways of what is always in danger of being lost. James VanDerZee's entire life's work was literally in jeopardy of being lost when Reginald McGhee discovered it in the back room of VanDerZee's studio in December 1967. Had VanDerZee not been discovered, would he have ever been missed? Perhaps not. But then it is just as true that in our ignorance our poverty would have been that much greater.

Joseph La Mar, circa 1907
Donna Mussenden VanDerZee

La Mar was James VanDerZee's
violin teacher in Lenox.

*Employees of the Aspinwall
Hotel, Lenox*, circa 1906
Donna Mussenden VanDerZee

Blacksmith shop, Phoebus, Virginia, 1908
Donna Mussenden VanDerZee

VanDerZee once said that he had been thinking about Henry Wadsworth Longfellow's poem "The Village Blacksmith" when he took this photograph.

Two soldiers (Needham Roberts and Henry Johnson), 1920
Prairie View A&M University, Texas

The American soldiers Henry Johnson (left) of Albany, New York, and
Needham Roberts (right) of Trenton, New Jersey, received the French
Croix de Guerre for bravery in battle in World War I, and VanDerZee
photographed them together when they returned to the United States and
again in 1932 (see page 142).

Lester A. Walton, date unknown
Donna Mussenden VanDerZee

Lester Walton (1882–1965) began his journalistic career in his hometown of St. Louis. From 1908 to 1914 he was drama critic and managing editor of the *New York Age*, one of the most widely read African American newspapers of the day. From 1914 to 1922, he was manager of the Lafayette Theater at Seventh Avenue and 132nd Street. Under his management the black musical-comedy revived and Harlem's first legitimate theater group, The Lafayette Players, was born. In the 1930s Walton was appointed ambassador to Liberia.

Police officer, 1924
The Metropolitan Museum of Art, New York; gift of the James VanDerZee Institute, 1970 (1970.539.21)

*Pledges of the Unity Athletic
and Social Club*, 1923
Donna Mussenden VanDerZee

A prophet, 1922
Donna Mussenden VanDerZee

In Harlem during the 1920s and
1930s, there were many spiritual-
ists, numerologists, magicians,
and other practitioners of the
occult. Many dressed in ornate
robes and turbans and carried
staffs.

Couple, 1924
Howard Greenberg Gallery, New
York City

Identical twins, 1924
The Metropolitan Museum of
Art, New York; gift of the James
VanDerZee Institute, 1970
(1970.539.2)

Portrait of a woman, 1924
Howard Greenberg Gallery, New
York City

Marcus Garvey in a UNIA Parade, 1924
Spike Lee

Marcus Moziah Garvey (1887–1940) was
born in St. Ann's Bay, Jamaica, and immi-
grated to America in 1916. In 1917, he organized the Universal Negro Improvement
Association, with its rallying cry of
"Africa for the Africans," and a year later
he launched *The Negro World*, a pan-Afri-
can weekly newspaper. At the height of its
strength, in 1921, the UNIA attracted more
than 25,000 people to Madison Square
Garden from around the world for its International Convention and succeeded in
building a mass movement among African
Americans throughout this country. By the
mid-1920s, the movement began to unravel
as Garvey experienced legal difficulties.

Marcus Garvey (right) with George O. Marke (left)
and Prince Kojo Tovalou-Houenou, 1924
Donna Mussenden VanDerZee

Prince Kojo Tovalou-Houenou of Dahomey was the editor of the Paris-based black-nationalist newspaper *Les
Continents* and was called the "Garvey of Africa": he
addressed the 1924 UNIA convention. The movement
had some fourteen hundred separate branches, more
than half of which were located in the United States and
Canada, with the others scattered throughout the Caribbean, Central and South America, and Africa. Supreme
Deputy George O. Marke was one of the UNIA's top
officials in 1924.

The staff of the UNIA news-paper, The Negro World, 1924
Donna Mussenden VanDerZee

Black Cross nurses watching a UNIA parade on Seventh Avenue, 1924
The Studio Museum in Harlem Archives, James VanDerZee Photographic Collection; and the Donna VanDerZee Collection

The Black Cross nurses were an auxiliary unit of the UNIA.

A member of Garvey's African Legion with his family, 1924
Martin Fine Art Photography,
Chevy Chase, Maryland

Garvey at Liberty Hall, 1924
Donna Mussenden VanDerZee

The UNIA's Liberty Hall on West 138th Street was described as "a low-roofed, hot, zinc-covered building that held 6,000 persons." Garvey himself sat on a dais at the front of the hall.[95]

Garveyites at UNIA headquarters, August 21, 1926
Donna Mussenden VanDerZee

The *Negro World* described the climactic scene when the New York Division of the UNIA held a rally for Garvey, who was in the Atlanta penitentiary: "At the top of the headquarter's steps was held aloft a life-sized portrait of Marcus Garvey which had been carried in the procession, and the eyes of all, streetcar motorman and policeman, truckman and passer-by, ardent member and erstwhile critic, were trained on this, as a band played the Ethiopian National Anthem and The Star Spangled Banner, and cheers for the absent leader rent the air."[96]

Renaissance Big Five Basketball Team, 1925
Spike Lee

One of the first black basketball teams, the Renaissance Big Five, was organized in 1923 by Robert Douglas, a Harlem player from the West Indies. During the 1920s and 1930s, they toured the United States, playing about 130 games a year and winning almost all of them. On the road, the team had to cope with pervasive racism and segregation, but it stayed together and prospered, gaining a reputation for clean, skillful play. The Renaissance Casino, which first sponsored the team, was located at 138th Street and Seventh Avenue and was operated by a black-owned realty company.

Dancer, 1925
Donna Mussenden VanDerZee

Two women in gypsy costumes,
1925
Howard Greenberg Gallery, New
York City

Portrait of a man, circa 1925
Donna Mussenden VanDerZee

Woman in a beaded dress, 1925
The Metropolitan Museum of
Art, New York; gift of the James
VanDerZee Institute, 1970
(1970.539.13)

The Sexteto Habanero, 1926
Donna Mussenden VanDerZee

The Latino community in Harlem was small in the 1920s. The music of the Sexteto Habanero was called Danzon: music to dance by.

Beau of the Ball, 1926
Donna Mussenden VanDerZee

Harlem had a lively gay subculture between the wars. This dignified portrait of a cross-dresser is done without any cultural or moral bias. In an interview with Jervis Anderson, Romare Bearden recalled a female impersonator named Gladys Bentley who sang at the Clam House on West 133rd Street, and another named Gloria Swanson: "Harlem was like Berlin, where they had such things going on in cabarets at the time."[99]

Family portrait, 1926
Donna Mussenden VanDerZee

*Alpha Phi Alpha basketball
team*, 1926
The Studio Museum in Harlem
Archives, James VanDerZee
Photographic Collection; and
Donna VanDerZee Collection

Alpha Phi Alpha was the first
intercollegiate Greek-letter fra-
ternity established for black
students.

Dinner party with boxer Harry Wills, 1926
The Studio Museum in Harlem Archives, James VanDerZee Photographic Collection

Harry Wills was a celebrated fighter in the 1920s — he was called "The Black Panther" — and after his retirement in 1932 he became one of Harlem's most respected businessmen, owning property throughout the community. He and his wife lived on Strivers' Row, a group of 106 houses on tree-lined 138th and 139th streets between Seventh Avenue and Eighth Avenue built for wealthy whites by a developer in 1891. By the end of the First World War, African American lawyers, doctors, writers, musicians, and businessmen and their families had begun to move into the stately houses, earning for them the name bestowed by less well-to-do Harlemites.

Florence Mills, 1927
Donna Mussenden VanDerZee

Singer and dancer Florence Mills (1895–1927) made
her stage debut at the age of eight in her hometown of
Washington, D.C. Fame came to her in 1921, when as a
chorus girl she upstaged the rest of the cast in the
musical *Shuffle Along.* A string of successes was
capped by her 1926 appearance in *Blackbirds,* which
she took to London and Paris after a run in New York
(including performances in Harlem as well as on
Broadway). She died shortly after her triumphal return to the States (see page 17).

Society Ladies, 1927
Donna Mussenden VanDerZee

This photograph was taken in a
home on Strivers' Row, on West
138th Street (VanDerZee's client
was a Mrs. Edith Milburn).

Baptism celebration, 1927
Howard Greenberg Gallery, New
York City

Wedding portrait, 1927
Donna Mussenden VanDerZee

Distributing the Chicago De-
fender, 1928
The Metropolitan Museum of
Art, New York; gift of the James
VanDerZee Institute, 1970
(1970.539.54)

The *Defender* was the first black
newspaper with a national
readership.

Street scene, date unknown
Donna Mussenden VanDerZee

Tea time at Madame C. J. Walker's Beauty Salon, 1929
The Metropolitan Museum of Art, New York; gift of the James VanDer-
Zee Institute, 1970 (1970.539.10)

Sarah Breedlove Walker (1867–1919), popularly known as Madame C. J.
Walker, was orphaned at the age of six, married at fourteen, and became
a widow with a young daughter at twenty. Starting with virtually nothing, she developed a hair product that proved to be commercially successful. By 1910 she had set up the Walker Manufacturing Company in
Indianapolis to produce her products. At the height of her success, she
had more than 2,000 sales agents. In 1914 she moved to Harlem, bought
two houses on West 136th Street, and established the Walker College of
Hair Culture.

The Barefoot Prophet, 1929
Donna Mussenden VanDerZee

Born in Henry County, Virginia, in 1851, the almost seven-foot-tall
Elder Clayhorn Martin was affectionately known as the Barefoot
Prophet. At an early age he had had a vision and a voice had told him to
"take off your shoes, for this is Holy Ground. Go Preach My Gospel."
He never wore shoes again. The Barefoot Prophet never had a church of
his own, but he preached on Harlem street corners and frequented
barbershops, cabarets, bars, restaurants, and house-rent parties spread-
ing the word of the Gospel.

Rabbi Matthew seated in the window of the Beth B'nai Abraham Synagogue, 29 West 131st Street, 1929
The Studio Museum in Harlem Archives, James VanDerZee Photographic Collection; and the Donna VanDerZee Collection

Wentworth Arthur Matthew was, with Arnold Josiah Ford, the leader of the Beth B'nai Abraham Synagogue of Black Jews, established in 1924. He had been a professional boxer and wrestler, and claimed to be a native of Sierra Leone who had traveled and studied in the Middle East. After the synagogue collapsed in 1930, Matthew reorganized the sect as The Commandment Keepers of the Living God.[101]

Wedding party, circa 1929
Donna Mussenden VanDerZee

The Dark Tower, circa 1929
The Studio Museum in Harlem Archives, James VanDerZee Photographic Collection.

In 1928, A'Lelia Walker established a literary salon, which she named after Countee Cullen's column in *Opportunity* magazine: "The Dark Tower." She dedicated a floor of her Harlem mansion at 108 West 136th Street—one of the townhouses purchased by her mother, Madame C. J. Walker, in 1914—to Harlem's artists and writers. Painted on the walls of one of the large rooms were poems: Countee Cullen's "The Dark Tower" and Langston Hughes's "The Weary Blues." Walker is not in this photograph.

Portrait of a woman, 1930
Donna Mussenden VanDerZee

VanDerZee etched the image of
the ring onto the negative.

Portrait of a man, 1931
Donna Mussenden VanDerZee

My Corsage, 1931
The Studio Museum in Harlem
Archives, James VanDerZee
Photographic Collection; and the
Donna VanDerZee Collection

Smart Cat, 1931
Donna Mussenden VanDerZee

Woman playing a ukelele, 1931
The Metropolitan Museum of
Art, New York; gift of the James
VanDerZee Institute, 1970
(1970.539.35)

Many of VanDerZee's studio
portraits include musical notes,
etched by hand on the negative,
that symbolically express the sitter's interest in music.

Queen of Swastika, 1932
Donna Mussenden VanDerZee

This portrait was taken a few
years before the black swastika
on a white circle with a crimson
background became the national
flag of Nazi Germany. A symbol
of prosperity and good fortune,
the swastika was used by a
number of organizations prior to
its becoming an infamous symbol
of evil.

Wedding portrait, 1931
Dr. Regenia A. Perry

B.P.O.E. Monarch Lodge No. 45
("Elks Home"), 1931
Donna Mussenden VanDerZee

VanDerZee was a member of the
Elks.

Needham Roberts, 1932
The Studio Museum in Harlem
Archives, James VanDerZee
Photographic Collection; and the
Donna VanDerZee Collection

A man in his bedroom, 1931
Donna Mussenden VanDerZee

Frances Williams at home after
being installed as head of the
Manhattan Temple Bible Club,
1932
Donna Mussenden VanDerZee

Altar boy, date unknown
Donna Mussenden VanDerZee

Communion Day portrait, 1933
Donna Mussenden VanDerZee

"Sunset and even star,
And one clear call for me,
When I put out to sea.
And may there be no moaning of the
bar,
Twilight and even bell,
And after than the dark.

"And may there be no sadness or fare-
well,
When I embark.
For tho' from out of bourne of time
and place,
The floods may bear me far,
I hope to see my Pilot face to face
When I have crossed the bar.

Memorial to Rachel VanDerZee,
1927
Donna Mussenden VanDerZee

Rachel VanDerZee died at the age of nineteen from peritonitis. Her obituary in the *New York Age* portrayed her as being "well known in Harlem as a basketball player and a member of the Cheerful Contributors Club, an organization of young high school girls and debutants doing social service in Harlem."[102]

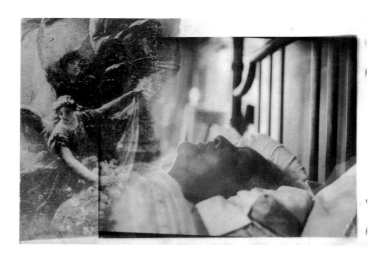

LEFT:
Susan VanDerZee, the photographer's Mother, 1931
Donna Mussenden VanDerZee

BELOW:
Mortuary portrait of an infant, 1928
Donna Mussenden VanDerZee

"Mostly, I made the death portraits in funeral parlors. . . . The portrait lenses were not good for those portraits; they gave more roundness and softness, not so much detail. People wanted sharp pictures for the funeral portraits."[103]

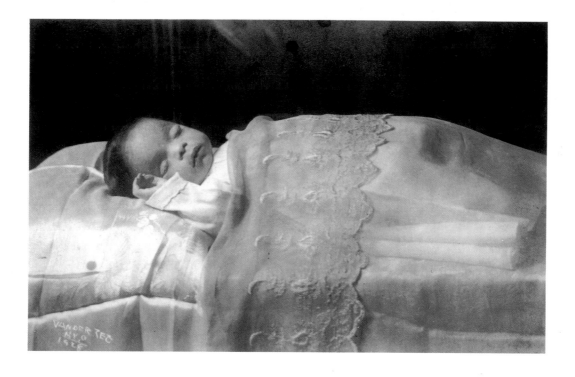

Mortuary portrait, 1931
Donna Mussenden VanDerZee

The Last Good-bye — Overseas,
circa 1941
Donna Mussenden VanDerZee

Mortuary portrait, 1941
Donna Mussenden VanDerZee

According to VanDerZee, the father is mourning over his son, who died after being struck by an automobile.[104]

Death of the first born, date
unknown
Donna Mussenden VanDerZee

The Hotel Theresa, 1933
The Studio Museum in Harlem Archives, James VanDerZee Photographic
Collection

During the 1930s, when blacks were first admitted as guests, the elegant
Hotel Theresa at Seventh Avenue and 125th Street became a Harlem
landmark.

Billiard Room, date unknown
The Studio Museum in Harlem
Archives, James VanDerZee
Photographic Collection

Two actors, 1933
Donna Mussenden VanDerZee

Children's theater group, date
unknown
The Studio Museum in Harlem
Archives, James VanDerZee
Photographic Collection; and the
Donna VanDerZee Collection

*Jack Johnson signing a contract with Frank Schiffman for
an appearance at the Apollo Theater*, 1933
Spike Lee

The American boxer Jack (John Arthur) Johnson (1878–
1946) was the first black heavyweight champion of the world,
a title that he finally won in 1908, causing an international
furor and excitement in black communities. He lost the title
in 1915, but continued to fight exhibition bouts until his death
in 1946 in an automobile accident. Impresario Frank Schiffman launched, with partner Leo Brecher, the legendary
Apollo Theater on 125th Street between Seventh and Eighth
Avenues, which opened under his management in January
1934. VanDerZee was evidently not impressed with Johnson:
"He came one time to our house on Lenox Avenue looking for
a room. It seems our prices were too high for him."[105]

Sam Langford with a promoter of the Grand National fights,
1936
The Metropolitan Museum of Art, New York; gift of the
James VanDerZee Institute, 1970 (1970.539.19)

Sam Langford (1886–1956) was born in Weymouth, Nova
Scotia. Nicknamed "The Boston Tar Baby," he fought 252
professional bouts but never won a title. The men are standing in front of the Tree of Hope, which stood on the island on
Seventh Avenue in front of the Lafayette Theater at 132nd
Street. It served as a good luck emblem for out-of-work Harlemites, who would regularly rub it in hope of finding em-
ployment. When the original tree died — its stump is visible
in this photograph — Bill Robinson contributed a new one,
which is now also gone. In 1972, a sculpture by Algernon
Miller was put in its place.

Three generations, 1934
Donna Mussenden VanDerZee

Flying Ace (Hubert Fauntleroy Julian),
1934
Donna Mussenden VanDerZee

Hubert Fauntleroy Julian was a Trini-
dadian who enlisted with the Royal Ca-
nadian Air Corps in World War I. He
later moved to Harlem, where he became
an officer in the UNIA. He parachuted
twice, in 1922 and 1923, into Harlem, the
second time while playing a gold-plated
saxophone; he missed his target each
time. He became a popular hero and the
New York Telegram dubbed him "The
Black Eagle." In 1930, Haile Selassie
chose him to head Ethiopia's Imperial
Air Force.

Monte Carlo Sporting Club, 1934
Donna Mussenden VanDerZee

Les Modernes Bridge Club, 1936
Donna Mussenden VanDerZee

Bill Robinson with child star Sunshine Sammy on his shoulders in front of the Harlem branch of the YMCA, 180 West 135th Street, date unknown
Donna Mussenden VanDerZee

Sunshine Sammy played in some of Harold Lloyd's silent movies.

Bill "Bojangles" Robinson, date unknown
Donna Mussenden VanDerZee

Bill Robinson (1878–1949) began dancing professionally at the age of eight. For nearly four decades, he was the foremost tap dancer on Broadway and a beloved figure in Harlem. Unlike other tap dancers, Robinson eschewed metal taps for wooden soles, and his easy style earned him his nickname. He appeared in several Hollywood movies, most memorably dancing with Shirley Temple in *The Little Colonel* and *The Littlest Rebel*.

Hazel Scott, 1936
Donna Mussenden VanDerZee

Jazz pianist Hazel Scott (1920–1981) moved to New
York from Trinidad at the age of four; a year later she
was taking piano lessons. As a teenager she played in her
mother's orchestra, the American Creolians (also known
as Alma Long Scott's All Girl Band). She first appeared
professionally as a jazz soloist with Count Basie in 1935,
and soon she had her own radio series and was a star
attraction in New York nightclubs. She toured widely
and appeared in musicals and films, including *Tropic-
ana* (1943), *I Dood It!* (1943), and *Rhapsody in Blue*
(1945), among others. She was married to Adam Clayton Powell, Jr., in 1945.

Portrait of a man, date unknown
The Studio Museum in Harlem
Archives, James VanDerZee
Photographic Collection; and the
Donna VanDerZee Collection

A bride, 1937
The Metropolitan Museum of
Art, New York; gift of the James
VanDerZee Institute, 1970
(1970.539.4)

Father Divine presiding over an outdoor banquet, circa 1938
The Studio Museum in Harlem Archives, James VanDerZee Photographic Collection; and the Donna VanDerZee Collection

Born George Baker in the American South, Father Divine (circa 1880–1965) settled in 1919 in Sayville, Long Island. In 1933 he moved to Harlem, where he presided over "Heaven," his Peace Mission at 20 West 155th Street. In the midst of the Great Depression, he would not permit his followers to accept public relief, and none went hungry. William Pickens, visiting Heaven in 1940, described a meal for readers of the *New York Age:* "The Father sits at the center of the head table, and there are two long tables reaching out from it . . . to the far end of the hall. All the food, every dish and every cup of it, passed by him; he touches the dishes with his hands, thus blessing the food."[106]

Daddy Grace, circa 1938
Amon Carter Museum, Fort Worth, Texas

Marcelino Manuael da Graca (1884–1960) was born in Brava, Cape
Verde Islands. His church in Harlem was called the United House of
Prayer for All People and he attracted many followers with his evange-
listic and fundamentalist preaching and services noted for being highly
charged and testimonial in style. An entrepreneur as well, he sponsored a
variety of products, including toothpaste and Daddy Grace's Sumptuous
Cookies. VanDerZee believed that he had "made quite a lot of money. He
is thought to have owned a large apartment building."[107]

At Home, 1934
Donna Mussenden VanDerZee

Josephine Becton was the widow of George Wilson Becton (1890–1933), who was, aside from Father Divine, the most noted evangelist in Harlem. Becton's ministry, the World Gospel Feast Party, Inc., attracted thousands, who contributed a dime a day to the cause, making him a wealthy man with real-estate holdings throughout Harlem. His luxurious apartment became the stuff of popular legend. He was kidnapped and murdered by gangsters in Philadelphia in 1933. His wife established the Becton Spiritualist Chapel as a memorial to her late husband and became a philanthropist.

The Heiress, 1938
The Museum of Modern Art,
New York City; Family of Man
Fund

After working for a wealthy
white family for many years, this
woman inherited their home and
furnishings.

*The Manhattan Temple Bible
Club Lunchroom,* 1936
The Metropolitan Museum of
Art, New York; gift of the James
VanDerZee Institute, 1970
(1970.539.53)

Man reading Life *magazine,*
1938
Donna Mussenden VanDerZee

Reclining nude, date unknown
The Metropolitan Museum of
Art, New York; gift of the James
VanDerZee Institute, 1970
(1970.539.30)

Women with Bouquet of Roses,
1938
The Metropolitan Museum of
Art, New York; gift of the James
VanDerZee Institute, 1970
(1970.539.48)

Father's Footsteps, 1935
Donna Mussenden VanDerZee

Father's Day, 1939
Donna Mussenden VanDerZee

A cleric, 1941
Dr. Regenia A. Perry

A soldier, 1944
The Metropolitan Museum of
Art, New York; gift of the James
VanDerZee Institute, 1970
(1970.539.24)

Couple, date unknown
Alfred Forrest and Eloise
Skelton-Forrest

Eubie Blake, 1981
Donna Mussenden VanDerZee

Musician and composer Eubie Blake (1883–1983) was almost the exact
contemporary of James VanDerZee. Born in Baltimore, Blake began
performing professionally at seventeen, becoming early a presence in the
nascent black music scene in New York. He teamed up with Noble Sissle,
and in 1915 they sold their first song, "It's All Your Fault," to Sophie
Tucker. Their 1921 Broadway musical comedy *Shuffle Along*, with hit
songs "I'm Just Wild About Harry" and "Love Will Find a Way," was a
watershed event in show business, and led to a string of productions.
During World War II, Blake was the musical conductor for the United
Services Organization (USO) Hospital Unit, and he continued to play
gigs until his death.

Bill Cosby, 1980
Donna Mussenden VanDerZee

Comedian, actor, and producer,
Philadelphian Bill Cosby (b.
1937) is probably the best-known
black entertainer in America. He
is an avid art collector and has
published numerous books and
records.

Lou Rawls, 1980
Donna Mussenden VanDerZee

The portrait of rhythm and blues
artist Lou Rawls was commis-
sioned for an album cover.

Ossie Davis and Ruby Dee, 1982
Donna Mussenden VanDerZee

Ossie Davis (b. 1917) and Ruby
Dee (b. 1924) have worked
together in the theater since 1946,
when they performed in the
American Negro Theater production of *Jeb.* They have appeared, both separately and
together, in numerous plays and
movies, most recently in Spike
Lee's *Do The Right Thing*
(1989) and *Jungle Fever* (1991).

184

Max Robinson, 1981
Donna Mussenden VanDerZee

News correspondent Max Robinson (1939–1988) joined ABC
World News Tonight in 1978 as
head of the National Desk in
Chicago. He was the first black
network anchorman to broadcast
regularly from a city other than
New York or Washington.

Romare Bearden, 1981
Donna Mussenden VanDerZee

Born in North Carolina, artist
Romare Bearden (1911–1988)
grew up in Harlem in a house
regularly visited by Duke El-
lington, Fats Waller, and Langston Hughes. Chiefly known as a
painter and collage artist, he also
had a career as a songwriter in
the 1950s.

Muhammad Ali, 1981
Donna Mussenden VanDerZee

Muhammad Ali, born Cassius Clay in 1942 in Louisville, Kentucky, took the world heavyweight boxing title in 1964 and held it on and off until 1979, when he retired with a record of fifty-six wins and three losses. Like Jack Johnson and Joe Louis before him, he became, at a young age, a hero in the black community. In 1963, he joined the Nation of Islam, and four years later he refused to serve in the armed forces on the grounds of his religious beliefs. He was indicted for draft evasion and sentenced to five years in prison, but in 1971 the United States Supreme Court overturned the indictment.

Jean-Michel Basquiat, 1982
Donna Mussenden VanDerZee

Jean-Michel Basquiat, born in 1960 in Brooklyn, became a graffiti artist
using the tag SAMO (for "same old shit") in 1977. He became involved
in the New York avant-garde art scene, and had a meteoric career as a
painter. His first solo exhibition in Modena, Italy, in 1981, was followed
by numerous others at home and abroad, and his work, which had many
admirers, became a lightning rod for some art critics. He died of a drug
overdose in 1988. After this sitting in 1982, Basquiat painted VanDer-
Zee's portrait.

NOTES

Self-portrait, 1918
Donna Mussenden VanDerZee

1. A. D. Coleman. "We Need More 'Dancing at the Savoy,'" *New York Times*, October 24, 1971.

2. bell hooks, *Black Looks: Race and Representation* (Boston, 1992), p. 7.

3. Mary Schmidt Campbell, "Introduction" in *Harlem Renaissance: Art of Black America* (New York, 1987), p. 36.

4. Reginald McGhee, *The World of James VanDerZee: A Visual Record of Black Americans* (New York, 1969), n.p.

5. Jim Haskins, *James VanDerZee: The Picture-Takin' Man* (New York, 1979), p. 166.

6. James Baldwin, *Nobody Knows My Name* (New York, 1961), p. 29.

7. John Gable, *A History of Trinity Church, Lenox, Massachusetts, 1763–1966* (North Adams, Mass., 1966), p. 39.

8. "Black Biography," n.d., n.p. Typescript in author's possession. This is a transcription of the interview James VanDerZee gave to Reginald McGhee in 1969.

9. Stanley Joseph, "Across the High Hills: Notes on Hudson Valley Blacks in Colonial Massachusetts," *The Columbian Repository* (Fall 1990), pp. 1–2. On the history of African Americans in New Baltimore see F.K.D., "Free Persons of Color," in n.a., *The Heritage of New Baltimore* (New Baltimore, New York, 1976), pp. 114–116.

10. Gable, *A History of Trinity Church*, p. 40.

11. W.E. Woodward, *Meet General Grant* (New York, 1928), p. 477.

12. Haskins, *James VanDerZee*, p. 27.

13. Ibid., pp. 37–38.

14. Interview with James VanDerZee, December 9, 1978. Hereafter cited as RCB/JVDZ.

15. Haskins, *James VanDerZee*, pp. 47–48.

16. RCB/JVDZ.

17. Haskins, *James VanDerZee*, p. 53.

18. Ibid., p. 52.

19. Ibid., p. 59.

20. Ibid., p. 60.

21. N.a., "Phoebus and the Freedom Fort," *The Appraisal* (March 1979), p. 2.

22. N.a., "The Castle Within," *The Cavalier* (January 1905), p. 14.

23. Francis Peabody, *Education for Life: The Story of Hampton Institute* (Garden City, New York, 1918), pp. 99–100, and Robert F. Engs, "Red, Black, and White: A Study in Intellectual Inequality," in *Region, Race, and Reconstruction*, eds. J. Morgan Kousser and James M. McPherson (New York, 1982).

24. For a history of the preparatory school see Helen W. Ludlow, *The Evolution of the Whittier School* (Hampton, Virginia, 1906).

25. Haskins, *James VanDerZee*, p. 61.

26. The most thorough studies of late-nineteenth-century Harlem and the black migration there in the twentieth century are: Seth Scheiner, *Negro Mecca, A History of the Negro in New York City, 1865–1920* (New York, 1965), pp. 35–38 and Gilbert Osofsky, *Harlem: The Making of a Ghetto*, rev. ed. (New York, 1971), pp. 71–120.

27. Camille Billops, "James VanDerZee Transcript," August 8, 1977. Typescript in the Hatch-Billops Collection.

28. Candice VanEllison, "Interview with James VanDerZee," in McGhee, *The World of James VanDerZee*, n.p. VanDerZee incorrectly dated his stay in Newark in this interview.

29. VanDerZee's studio practices were congruent, for example, with the successful Bachrach Studios. See n.a., *A History of Bachrach: Being an Account of the Notable Applications of the Principles of Art and Business to Photography* (Newton, Mass., 1927), pp. 5–10, 17–25, and 26–34.

30. Wedding certificate, James VanDerZee and Gaynella Greenlee.

31. Haskins, *James VanDerZee*, p. 97.

32. Ibid., p. 104.

33. Several scholars have written about the post–World War I era in Harlem and the various expressions of African American culture there. Among the best are: Nathan Huggins,

Harlem Renaissance (New York, 1979), especially pp. 52–83, and David L. Lewis, *When Harlem Was in Vogue* (New York, 1979), pp. 89–118. See also Cary D. Wintz, *Black Culture and the Harlem Renaissance* (Houston, Texas, 1988), pp. 30–47.

34. For example, in 1937 Myrtle E. Pollard listed three: William E. Woodard at 2386 Seventh Avenue, Vernon and King on 135th Street, and Winifred Hall, "the only female of color," also on Seventh Avenue. See Pollard, "Harlem As Is" (Master's thesis, City College of New York, 1937), vol. 2, pp. 258–260.

35. Estelle Jussim, "From the Studio to the Snapshot: An Immigrant Photographer of the 1920s," *History of Photography* (July 1977), p. 192 and Val Williams, *Women Photographers: The Other Observers, 1900 to the Present* (London, 1986), pp. 142–166.

36. Cynthia Wayne, *Dreams, Lies, and Exaggerations: Photomontage in America*, exh. cat., University of Maryland Art Gallery, October 21–December 20, 1991, pp. 34 and 68–71.

37. Rodger C. Birt, "For the Record: James VanDerZee, Marcus Garvey, and the UNIA Photographs," *International Review of African American Art*, 8 (No. 4), pp. 39–48.

38. On business success and failure in Harlem during the depression see Roi Otley and William Weatherly, eds., *The Negro in New York: An Informal Social History, 1626–1940* (New York, 1967), p. 237.

39. The information on the VanDerZees' business activities during this period is in the files of James VanDerZee's widow, Donna Mussenden VanDerZee (hereafter cited as VDZFILE).

40. Cecil Beaton, *Cecil Beaton's New York* (Philadelphia, 1938), pp. 170–180.

41. The history of 272 Lenox Avenue is recorded in the Office of the City Registrar (New York, New York); Block 1721, Lot 73.

42. "Black Biography," n.d., n.p.

43. The most cogent discussion of this phenomenon in Harlem and other cities with large black populations is in William J. Wilson, *The Truly Disadvantaged: The Inner City, the Underclass, and Public Policy* (Chicago, 1987), pp. 20–62.

44. Advertisements and letters in VDZFILE.

45. This is the chronology of events leading up to the foreclosure of the last mortgage as reconstructed from the papers in VDZFILE.

46. Interview with Reginald McGhee, April 3, 1987 (hereafter cited as RCB/McGh).

47. Interview with Allon Schoener, January 23, 1987 (hereafter cited as RCB/AS).

48. *New York Times*, Nov. 16, 1967.

49. RCB/McGh.

50. RCB/AS.

51. Romare Bearden, letter to Allon Schoener, June 6, 1968. Copy in author's files.

52. Interview with Louise Broecker, April 15, 1987.

53. *New York Times*, Nov. 23, 1968.

54. Interview with Jean Hutson, May 7, 1987 (hereafter cited as RCB/JH).

55. RCB/AS.

56. Candice VanEllison, introduction in Allon Schoener, ed., *Harlem On My Mind: Cultural Capital of Black America, 1900–1968* (New York, 1968), n.p.

57. *New York Times*, Jan. 18, 1969.

58. *New York Times*, Jan. 29, 1969.

59. RCB/McGh.

60. *New York Times*, Jan. 15, 1969.

61. Jacob Deschin, "Harlem's History in Visual Survey," *New York Times*, January 19, 1969.

62. RCB/AS.

63. *New York Times*, Feb. 1, 1969.

64. *New York Amsterdam News*, Feb. 1, 1969.

65. RCB/JH.

66. *New York Post*, Jan. 23, 1969.

67. RCB/JH.

68. RCB/AS.

69. RCB/McGh.

70. *New York Times,* April 8, 1969, and April 9, 1969.

71. RCB/McGh. See also New York *Times,* April 8 and 9, 1969.

72. Reginald McGhee, *The World of James VanDerZee* (New York, 1969) and Liliane DeCock and Reginald McGhee, *James VanDerZee* (Dobbs Ferry, New York, 1973).

73. RCB/McGh.

74. Interview with Ruth Sherman, Nov. 20, 1986.

75. Six of these portraits were reproduced in *Black Art: An International Quarterly* (Summer 1977), pp. 44–49.

76. Interview with Camille Billops, January 21, 1987.

77. RCB/McGh.

78. James VanDerZee et al., *The Harlem Book of the Dead* (Dobbs Ferry, New York, 1978).

79. "The Legacy of James VanDerZee," Alternative Center for International Art, New York, Oct. 1–29, 1977.

80. *Weekend Big Red,* August 14, 1977.

81. Interview with Marvin Mansky.

82. Regenia Perry, *Roots in Harlem,* exh. cat. (Brooks Memorial Art Gallery, Memphis, 1989), p. 18.

83. Ibid., p. 19.

84. James VanDerZee, letter to Reginald McGhee, Nov. 16, 1977. Copy in author's files.

85. Affidavit of the Attorney General, Supreme Court of the State of New York, Index No. 1517/81, p. 4.

86. Haskins, *James VanDerZee,* p. 213.

87. See, for example, A. D. Coleman, *Light Readings: A Photography Critic's Writings, 1968–1978* (New York, 1979), p. 17.

88. McGhee, *The World of James VanDerZee,* n.p.

89. Beaumont Newhall, *The History of Photography,* rev. ed. (New York, 1982). It is worth noting that VanDerZee is included in what some would consider the "official" history of art albeit as a source of "great documentary value": H. W. Janson's *History of Art,* fourth ed. (New York, 1991), p. 801. See also Gene Thornton, "Why Harlem's James VanDerZee Isn't in the History Books," *New York Times,* Feb. 26, 1984.

90. Huggins, pp. 137–189 and Henry Louis Gates, Jr., "The Trope of a New Negro and the Reconstruction of the Image of the Black," *Representations* (Fall 1988), pp. 129–155.

91. Roland Barthes, *Camera Lucida: Reflections on Photography,* trans. Richard Howard (New York, 1981), pp. 43, 53, and 57.

92. Kelly Wise, ed., *Portrait Theory: Photography and Essays* (New York, 1982), p. 159.

93. Ibid., p. 158.

94. Haskins, *James VanDerZee,* p. 204.

95. Jervis Anderson, *This Was Harlem* (New York, 1982), p. 125.

96. *The Negro World,* August 21, 1926.

97. Anderson, *This Was Harlem,* p. 255.

98. Lewis, *When Harlem Was in Vogue,* p. 111.

99. Anderson, *This Was Harlem,* p. 169.

100. Haskins, *James VanDerZee,* p. 181.

101. Lewis, *When Harlem Was in Vogue,* pp. 222–3.

102. Haskins, *James VanDerZee,* p. 180.

103. Wise, *Portrait Theory,* p. 158.

104. VanDerZee, *The Harlem Book of the Dead* , p. 84.

105. Jerry Talmer, "A Memory from Harlem," *New York Post,* March 3, 1979, p. 33.

106. Quoted in Anderson, *This Was Harlem,* pp. 252–53.

107. Wise, *Portrait Theory,* p. 158.

BIBLIOGRAPHY

The following works deal in whole or in part with James VanDerZee:

Campbell, Mary Schmidt; Driskell, David; Lewis, David Levering; and Willis Ryan, Deborah. *Harlem Renaissance: Art of Black America*. New York: Harry N. Abrams, Inc. Publishers, 1987.

Coar, Valencia Hollins. *A Century of Black Photographers: 1840–1960*. Providence: Museum of Art, Rhode Island School of Design, 1983.

Haskins, Jim. *James VanDerZee: The Picture-Takin' Man*. Trenton, New Jersey: Africa World Press, Inc., 1991

McGhee, Reginald. *The World of James VanDerZee: A Visual Record of Black Americans*. New York: Grove Press, 1969.

Perry, Regenia. A., *James VanDerZee*. Dobbs Ferry, New York: Morgan and Morgan, 1973.

----------------- *Roots in Harlem: Photographs by James VanDerZee, from the Collection of Reginia A. Perry*. Catalogue. Memphis, Tennessee: Memphis Memorial Art Gallery, 1989.

VanDerZee, James; Billops, Camille; and Dodson, Owen. *The Harlem Book of the Dead: Photographs by James VanDerZee*. Dobbs Ferry, New York: Morgan and Morgan, 1978.

Willis-Thomas, Deborah. *Black Photographers, 1840–1940: An Illustrated Bio-Bibliography*. New York and London: Garland Publishing, Inc., 1985.